SAVE MONEY BUYING MEAT, POULTRY, AND FISH

by

Reggie the Butcher

Presidio Press

To my wife, Dee, who is my sweetheart, lover,
mother to my two great sons, nurse, world's
greatest cook, fantastic housekeeper, friend,
companion, lawyer, gardener, counselor,
bookkeeper, paymaster, banker, auditor,
and although she doesn't drive a car,
she tells me where to park.
But most of all she's my everything.

Copyright © 1981 by Reggie Leipsie
All rights reserved

Published by Presidio Press, 31 Pamaron Way, Novato, California 94947

Second edition, revised

Library of Congress Cataloging in Publication Data

Reggie the Butcher, 1913–
  Save money buying meat, poultry, and fish.

  Includes index.
  1. Meat. Poultry. 3. Fish as food. 4. Marketing (Home economics)
I. Title.
TX373.R42   641.3'6   80-25381

Illustrations by Tony Sommers

Edited by Joan Griffin

Printed in the United States

CONTENTS

This book would never have been published without the help of all these beautiful people:

My deep appreciation to the talented team at Presidio Press, who made me feel part of the family: to Senior Editor Joan Griffin for her outstanding efforts in taking a manuscript that was ''a field of weeds'' and creating ''a garden of roses''; and to Adele Horwitz and Ernest Pinkerton, for their faith in me.

To my friends at KGO radio: Owen Spann for his encouragement and enthusiasm; Hap Kaufman, who gave me my first break; and Al Collins, for all those plugs.

To Rita Cohen of KNEW radio, and to Bob Lipman and Bob Nathan of KTOB radio, for radio time and encouragement.

My thanks for the contributors of information and recipes: American Lamb Council, National Pork Producers Council, National Livestock and Meat Board, Beef Council, Delft Blue-Provimi Inc., California Turkey Industry Board, U.S. Department of Agriculture, University of California—Division of Agriculture Sciences, National Oceanic and Atmospheric Administration, National Marine Fisheries Service. And to my faithful radio listeners, who sent in tips and money-saving recipes.

To Mr. and Mrs. Art Cader, who gave me the courage to keep trying; to Joe Harrosh, who made me work harder; and to Jud Snider for his constructive criticism.

To Al Geraldi, "The World's Greatest Butcher," who took me under his wing and trained me in the fundamentals of the meat business.

To Tony Sommers, my illustrator, for the outstanding drawings that make the book come alive.

And to all my family, who made the book worth writing.

PREFACE

I've been in the meat business since 1937, and I've found that many people really don't know how to get the most for their money.

Everyone wants to save money, and when you buy meat there is a lot of it to be saved—if you know what you are doing.

Because I have an interest in people, and because I've worked in every phase of the meat industry, I realize that people need help in order to get the most for their money. But there are no books on how to do it. There's a lot of books about the names of meat cuts, how to sharpen your knives, and how to cook meat, but nothing on saving money when you buy it.

For years I've written down notes, talked to my customers, asked questions, more questions, and thought of ideas on how you can save money. Everyone I talked to, both men and women, agreed that it would be very beneficial for a butcher to compile ideas on how to save money buying meat.

So here it is, "My Way." I sincerely hope this system will save you money. This is the way I save money, and that's why I wrote this book.

Petaluma, California
1981

INTRODUCTION
GETTING THE SYSTEM ESTABLISHED

TODAY we are all looking for ways to beat high prices. That is what this book is all about. Meat is the principal item your meals are based upon, and it is the most expensive part of your food bill. But you *can* eat meat for less money.

I can recall countless times that I saved money for consumers by explaining to them how to get more meat for their money. And I made a lot of friends doing it. If you use my system, you buy the same meat everyone else buys, but you buy it for less. This may sound unbelievable, but it isn't. Let's look at what you have been doing:

YOUR WAY You want stew meat, so you buy a package labeled "stew meat." You want ground meat, so you pick it up out of the cooler and pay the price. You, your neighbor, and just about everyone else buys meat the same way. So, for example, you buy:

3 lbs. ground chuck at $2.39 a lb. = $ 7.17
1½ lbs. stew beef at $2.89 a lb. = $ 4.34
Total cost = $11.51

Now let's see how I would do it:

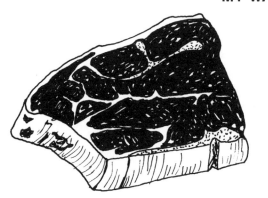

MY WAY I buy a 5 lb. seven-bone roast. I have the butcher grind 3 pounds and cut 1½ pounds into stew meat. I end up with same thing you bought, plus ½ pound of soup bones.

5 lb. chuck roast at $1.48 a lb. = $ 7.40

Your Way $11.51
My Way   7.40
SAVINGS $ 4.11

"Prices will change, but my system will never change and will always save you money."

You paid $4.11 more than I did for three things: *labor, service,* and *convenience.* Sometimes it might be worth it to you to pay this, for example, when you're in a hurry. But if you want to save this $4.11, learn to buy your meat "My Way."

The prices I use in this book are neither high nor low, but a happy average for USDA (U.S. Department of Agriculture) Choice meat in 1980. Prices will fluctuate from week to week, and will probably continue to rise, so the prices used in this book will change. But the *system* will not change. As the prices go up, your savings will go up too. Saving money when you buy meat is just a matter of knowing what to do. It is as simple as that.

Plan Ahead

Good, economical meals are planned at the table with a pencil and paper and the advertisements of the week's food specials. In most cities, supermarket ads appear on Wednesday. Look at them, compare, and decide which stores have the best buys. Always remember that you are about to make a very expensive purchase. Look for the best buys and you will come out ahead.

When you plan your meals, think in terms of two or three meals from one cut of meat. For example: steak, hamburger, and stew from a large chuck roast; a roast, steaks, and shish kebab from a leg of lamb. In general, you save when you buy the larger cuts of meat. If you are cooking for one or two people, you can *still* buy the larger cuts—just put the extra meat in your freezer (and put the extra money in the bank!).

"Never pay more for meat decorated with parsley."

Go to the supermarket with a list of what you need. Leave the kids at home: they distract you and wear you out, so you start rushing to get it over with. If you have to go to two or three stores to make the best buys, do so if you don't have to drive too many miles. Thursday is a very good day to shop because it is the second day of most sales and the merchandise is still on hand. Remember that sales usually run for one week. If the store is out of an item, be sure to get a "rain check"—this is a promise from the store that you'll be able to get the advertised item at the sale price when it is back in stock.

Know the Price of Meat

If you want to recognize good sale prices on meat, you must have a good idea of the regular prices. A shrewd buyer has a price list, either on paper or in her hand, so she knows a bargain when she sees one.

Get a small notebook. List the cuts of meat and what they normally cost per pound. With a knowledge of regular prices, you can check the advertisements and the meat counters and know a bargain when you see one. You will also recognize merchandising gimmicks like charging more for meat in fancy packaging. Never pay more for meat decorated with parsley!

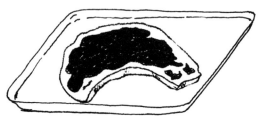 

Look for Quality

Don't buy on price alone. You also have to judge the quality of the meat. A bargain is a bargain only when the price is right *and* the quality is good. You must consider trim, marbling, bone, general appearance, and also grade and yield. Grade and yield are not shown on retail labels (this is one of my pet peeves), but you can ask the butcher. When the butcher buys his meat from the supplier, he must consider these very same things or he would soon be out of business.

TRIM   Look closely at the trim. You want to pay for meat, not fat. If there is more than ½ inch of fat around the outside of a steak or roast, pass it up.

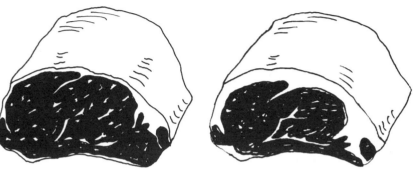

Also look at the size of the clod of fat in the porterhouse steak and in the rib steak.

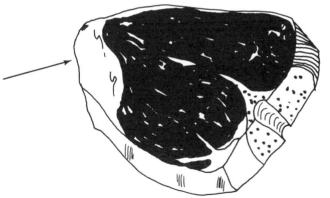

Keep your eye out for excessive bone, because you pay for it and then throw it away.

Avoid long tails in chops and steaks.

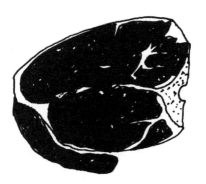 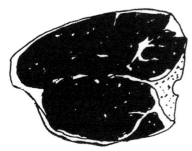

Beware of shops that give a bad trim when they put something on sale—for example, long tails and excessive fat on steaks. Although the price is lower, you get a bad bargain because the meat is not trimmed properly. If you find a market that does this, don't patronize it.

When you choose a piece of meat, be sure that part of it has not been cut out. Sometimes the most desirable piece will be cut out and sold separately for a higher price. This is occasionally done with chuck steaks, blade chuck roast, seven-bone roast, and full-cut round steak. To spot this rip-off, you must know what the cut of meat should look like in the first place. I'll show you what to watch for. If a piece has been cut out, ask the butcher to exchange the cut for another. If he refuses, find yourself another shop. You're paying the money—don't let them take advantage of you.

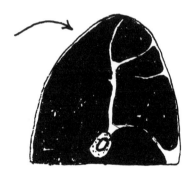

Full cut round steak

GENERAL APPEARANCE   Meat should look bright red. If it is dark or on the shady side, it was probably cut three or four days ago and is beginning to deteriorate.

Check for blood clots and bruises—they will be a darker color and will be soft and squishy. Don't you be the one to take them home.

Watch for "fretted" or "overheated" meat. You can recognize it by its dark red, crimson color. This happens when the animal is sweating, overheated, or nervous while being slaughtered. If you run into this, don't buy it, as it will be tough, dry, and chewy. Good markets send back overheated meat, but there are other shops that don't care.

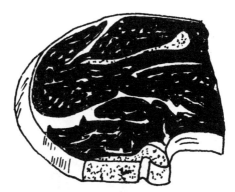

Chuck blade roast

MARBLING   Always look for the tiny flecks and streaks of fat that run through the meat. This is called *marbling,* and it makes the meat tender and flavorful. If a piece of meat is all red with no marbling, it was only grass fed. It will be tough, tasteless, and dry.

The USDA classifies degrees of marbling in meat: abundant, moderately abundant, slightly abundant, moderate, modest, small amount, slight amount, traces, practically devoid, and devoid. So you can see how very important marbling is.

If I told you a thousand times to check the marbling when you buy your meat, it still would not be enough. It is the best sign you can get of how the meat will cook and taste.

GRADING The USDA does an excellent job of looking out for you, the consumer, by *grading* meat. The grade is based on evaluation of two things:

> The percent of trimmed, boneless, major retail cuts that can be derived from the carcass; this is referred to as *yield grade*. The palatability of the lean meat; this is called *quality grade*.

The grading system depends on the kind of meat. Beef has more grade designations than lamb or pork because it varies more in quality. We'll discuss the different grading systems of various meats in later chapters.

Grading is done on a voluntary basis. Only about half of all meat sold is graded. Graded meat has a shield-like mark stamped on it in harmless vegetable dye. This grade is your guide to the tenderness, juiciness, and flavor of the meat. Some markets use ungraded meat and give it their own house name, which is confusing to the consumer. To discover the quality, you must use trial and error, and even then you'll find that the quality is not always consistent.

The *yield grade* is the ratio of lean meat to fat and bone. For example, the yield on a whole chicken weighing 2½ pounds is poor: there is a lot of frame and little meat. A 4-pound chicken has more meat on its frame, so it is a much better buy.

The determination of a yield grade on a beef carcass is based on the amount of external fat; the amount of kidney, pelvic, and heart fat; the size of the rib-eye muscle; and the carcass weight. Beef yield is judged according to the following grades:

Yield 1 - the carcass will yield 79.8% or more in retail cuts
Yield 2 - 75.2% to 79.7%
Yield 3 - 70.6% to 75.1%
Yield 4 - 66% to 70.5%
Yield 5 - 65.9% or less

Less than 5 percent of all beef is Yield 1; 25 percent is Yield 2; slightly more than 50 percent is Yield 3. Avoid Yield 3 if you can. There is less meat and more fat and bones.

Yield grades and quality grades are not identified on the retail label, but many markets post a notice of the grade of meat they carry. If they don't, ask the butcher. It is especially important to know about yield when you buy large cuts for your freezer. You can afford to pay more for a higher-yielding carcass, since you get

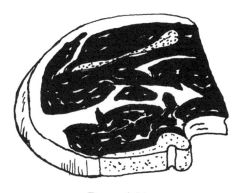

Poor yield   **Good yield**

more meat for your money. If there is no price differential, you get more for your money with the higher yield.

Meat that has passed federal inspection is marked with a round purple stamp. All meat processed in plants that sell products across state lines must be inspected by the USDA for wholesomeness.

Know Your Store's Service Policy

Each store has its own service policy, but they all provide some free services. To get the most for your money, you must know the policy of your store. As a test I once wrote to all the large chain

"Don't be afraid to ring the bell."

and independent supermarkets in the San Francisco Bay Area, asking what services their meat departments would provide for no additional cost. You would be surprised at how much they differed. Some stores do just about anything for you at no additional charge. Other stores are not so accommodating and charge you for all but the simplest things. Most are somewhere in between.

It is up to you to discover the policy for each store because they don't publicize it. Ask questions like:

> Will you slice a canned ham for no extra charge?
> Will you bone out a chuck roast and grind it for me?
> Cut a special steak?
> Cut a special roast?
> Will you cut a turkey into parts?
> If you do not have a certain item, will you order it for me?
> Do you give rain checks when you're out of advertised items?

It's important to know all this, because if your store won't provide these services, there are other shops that will. And insist that they follow their policy. Ring the bell and ask the butcher for help. Ask for that special cut. Don't take a package of three chops when you only want two. Insist on getting what you want, and you'll surely get your way.

If you ever get the runaround from the butcher, go to the store manager. He will tell you of the store policy on free services available, and will usually give you a refund if the meat is not satisfactory.

Consider Cutting Meat at Home

You can save a lot of money by learning how to do some of your own cutting and grinding at home. You wouldn't want to do the major cutting (the butcher does this quite efficiently on the electric saw), but sometimes you pay more for work that could be done easily at home—for example, cutting up chickens and turkeys, cutting chops and steaks from roasts, making cube steaks, grinding meat, and slicing meats. Sometimes your butcher will do these things for you, but sometimes he may be reluctant because he is too busy, or perhaps the store's policy is to charge for these additional services. That's the time to do it yourself, using my instructions.

As you learn to bone and cut meat at home, you will consistently improve your style. It's not easy at first, but gradually you will become a pro. Remember, when you buy packaged meat, you're paying for labor, service, and convenience. Do some cutting yourself and you can really save.

Chinese cleaver

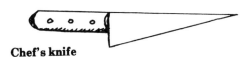

Chef's knife

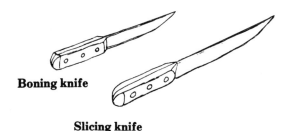

Boning knife

Slicing knife

Essential Equipment

KNIVES You can get along with just a few good knives: a five-inch boning knife, an eight-inch or ten-inch slicing knife, and a Chinese cleaver or chef's knife. I prefer a cleaver to a chef's knife because it is more versatile. A cleaver can be used for slicing and for cutting up stew meat. It is heavy enough to chop small bones, but maneuverable enough to be used like a knife. You can also use it for cutting vegetables. Here's a tip: when using a cleaver, hold it high up on the handle, putting your thumb and index finger on either side of the blade; this will stabilize the knife so it can't wobble.

Knives are made from different kinds of steel, and it's important to know what you're buying. Stainless steel knives look beautiful and require little care. They are extremely difficult to resharpen, however, because the steel is so hard. Carbon steel, on the other hand, is much softer and can be sharpened to a razor-like edge. But if not meticulously cared for these knives will rust, pit, and stain. I recommend high carbon stainless steel, which is the perfect compromise. This blend of steel holds an edge, can be resharpened easily, and also resists rusting and staining.

Keep your knives sharp. A dull knife is more dangerous than a sharp one because with a dull knife you must force the blade, using too much pressure. When you sharpen a knife, what you are actually doing is realigning the edge. To do this you use a sharpening stone or a steel, or both—whatever is recommended by the cutlery manufacturer. Be sure to read the instructions before sharpening your knives.

To use a sharpening stone, shake powdered cleanser on the stone and a little water to make a paste. This is a secret passed on to me by a professional knife-sharpener. Don't use oil—it clogs the pores of the stone. The cleanser provides a smooth, gliding surface, and cleans the stone in the process. Slide your knife to the left, to the right, then back again, holding it almost flat. Stone the knife first on the rough side of the stone, then on the smooth side.

"A dull knife is dangerous."

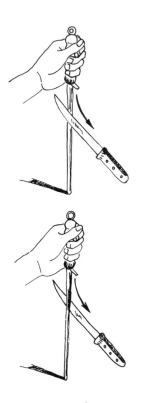

To use a steel, hold it by the handle, rest the point on the table and keep the steel straight up and down. This way it is impossible to cut your finger. Hold the knife at about a 20-degree angle with the blade down; if you hold it at too great an angle, it will dull your knife. Run the blade (from the heel to the tip) from the top of the steel to the bottom—first on the right side, then on the left.

Each time you use your knife, give it a few strokes on the steel. You'll find your cutting chores are easier and safer. With practice, you will soon feel comfortable sharpening your own knives. If you don't you can always have your knives professionally sharpened.

Always keep your knives in a sheath or in a storage block. There will be less chance of cutting yourself, and the blade will remain sharp. Always cut on a good-sized cutting board that has a well in it to save the juices. Cutting on a plate or a metal surface turns the edge of the knife blade. Never cut meat inside a frying pan. Not only does it ruin the cutting edge, but if the meat slips you can splatter yourself with hot grease. If you use teflon pans, the knife scores will ruin them.

My advice is to purchase all your tools at a butcher supply house if there is one in your area; they have good quality knives and an excellent selection. Fine cutlery is also sold in hardware stores, department stores, and gourmet shops—just remember: look for quality and don't be tempted by the lowest price.

FREEZER To save money buying meat on a family scale, you need a freezer —and I don't mean a freezer compartment in the refrigerator. If you think you can't afford one, this book shows you how to save enough money to buy one!

Don't think of a freezer simply as an appliance. It is also a tool to save money. Considering the bargains you can take advantage of, you cannot afford to be without one. If you don't believe me, ask the owner of a freezer. See what he or she tells you. Even after you pay for the electricity it takes to run the freezer, you'll still be ahead.

If the freezer is only a supplement to weekly shopping trips, three cubic feet for each member of the family is sufficient. If you prefer to buy in large quantities, you'll need six cubic feet for each member of your family. One cubic foot of freezer space will hold about 35 to 40 pounds of cut and wrapped meat.

Personally, I prefer an upright, self-defrosting, 20-cubic-foot freezer. No matter how large your family, this size is ideal. You can find packages faster in an upright freezer. The packages get less freezer burn because they are not piled on top of each other, so there's less chance of the wrapping getting ripped. Finally, your back will never ache from bending over.

A manual defrosting freezer is about $100 cheaper, so you might consider getting one. They have to be defrosted twice a year, which isn't really a hard job, considering the money you save.

When you buy a freezer, you immediately change your food-buying habits. Instead of getting one or two chickens at a sale, you get 12 or even 24—and instead of saving $0.20, you save $2.40 or $4.80. You can cash in on sales of other food as well—frozen vegetables, juices, bread, and so on.

It is a great idea to have a running inventory of everything you have in the freezer in the kitchen, pasted behind a cabinet door. When you use a package from the freezer, cross it off the inventory. When you buy, add to the inventory. Everyone in your family has to assist you religiously in this! This way, when you write your shopping list for specials and you see, for example, a sale on chuck roasts, you check your inventory. If you have 15 chuck roasts in the freezer, you'll probably want to pass on this sale and buy something else. It is no saving to buy too many of the same cuts.

TIP Remember, meat should be rewrapped if you're going to freeze it for a long time, so keep freezer paper and aluminum foil on hand.

Each package you put in the freezer should be marked and dated. This is important because the recommended time for storing each kind of meat is different. And if you keep meat too long, it will lose moisture and become dry and tasteless. Below is a list of times I recommend that you keep meat in the freezer.

Beef steaks and roasts	8 to 12 months
Lamb steaks and roasts	8 to 12 months
Veal steaks and roasts	4 to 8 months
Pork steaks and roasts	4 to 8 months
Chops: lamb, pork, veal	3 to 6 months
Ground beef, veal, lamb	3 to 4 months
Ground pork	1 to 3 months
Sausage	1 to 2 months
Stew meats	3 to 4 months
Chicken or turkey	12 months
Duck or goose	6 months
Giblets	3 months
Fried chicken	4 months
Cooked meat	2 to 3 months
Variety meats	3 to 4 months
Ham	1 to 2 months
Bacon	Less than 1 month
Corned beef and hot dogs	Less than 1 month
Luncheon meats	Freezing not recommended
Fresh fish	6 to 9 months
Frozen fish fillets and shrimp	3 to 4 months
Clams and cooked fish	3 months

The best months to fill your freezer are January, February, and March. Due to many factors—these are bad business months, and the dealers put on good sales. Thus you can cash in on low prices.

PACKAGED FREEZER SPECIALS: People always ask me about packaged freezer deals. They are good in some ways, bad in others.

ADVANTAGES: The meat is usually tender and choice. If the package of meat is tough, the dealer should replace it. And, you can have a lot of meat in your freezer at all times.

DISADVANTAGES: You don't see the meat being cut and ground. Do you know if you got a fair count on the weight? Let's say that you pay for 175 pounds of meat. About 20 percent to 30 percent is bones and fat. That leaves you with about 150 pounds of actual meat from the 175 pounds you paid for. Sometimes butchers add fat and bones in package deals and give you less meat. Also, you have no guarantee that you always get the best cuts. Not all dealers are dishonest, but some are. You have to be careful.

Unless you are very knowledgeable about meat, and unless you know your dealer is reliable, I'd advise you to stay away from freezer deals. You have comparable savings by buying sale items using the system that I use, and your freezer will be filled with the cuts of meat that you like.

OPTIONAL EQUIPMENT

Today many people grind meat with food processors. They are wonderful and can grind meat in seconds! But don't sell short the old hand grinder that your grandmother used—it's a great tool. You can save a lot of money by grinding your own meat.

You should also have a needle to sew up a boneless roast or a turkey.

A wooden mallet is a handy tool to have. You can save money by using this mallet to pound meat into thin slices, instead of paying high prices for thinly sliced meat, such as beef and veal for scallopini. Use a mallet without teeth to pound meat thin (or use your rolling pin!). For tenderizing meat use a mallet with teeth.

A stainless steel internal/external baster is also nice to have. It can be used to inject wine into a chicken or turkey (during the last 15 minutes in the oven), or inject butter and lemon juice into a leg of lamb. It can also save you money: you can tenderize cheaper cuts of meat by injecting lemon juice, wine, or vinegar into them.

If you can afford an electric meat slicer, you can save money by slicing your own ham, lunch meat, and salami, not to mention the fancier cuts of veal or beef for scallopini, stroganoff, and other fancy dishes.

Start Saving!

So, plan before you shop. Know the cuts you want before you talk to your butcher. Buy food value, not frills, fancy packages, or fancy names. Be willing to cut some of your own meat at home. Make your freezer work for you. Ask your butcher whenever you have questions. And use "My Way" of buying meat. It'll save you dollars and you'll get better cuts of meat.

BEEF

BEEF is America's favorite meat: 65 percent of the population likes it. You'll always find a good selection of cuts displayed in the supermarkets. Get to know the names of cuts of beef (see the chart) and avoid the slang names improvised by butchers and markets, such as Texas broil, fluff steak, Diamond Jim roast, California roast, Delmonico steak, watermelon roast, etc. These are not U.S. Department of Agriculture cuts. The USDA has standard names for every cut of meat. Learn and use them, and it will help you save money.

Some cuts of beef are more tender than others. Those from the less-used muscles along the back of the animal—such as the rib and loin—are quite tender; the active muscles—shoulder (chuck), flank, and round—are less tender. The tender cuts are only a small part of the animal and are in great demand, so they sell for a higher price. Chuck and round make up a large part of the animal, so they are cheaper. That's why you often see them on sale.

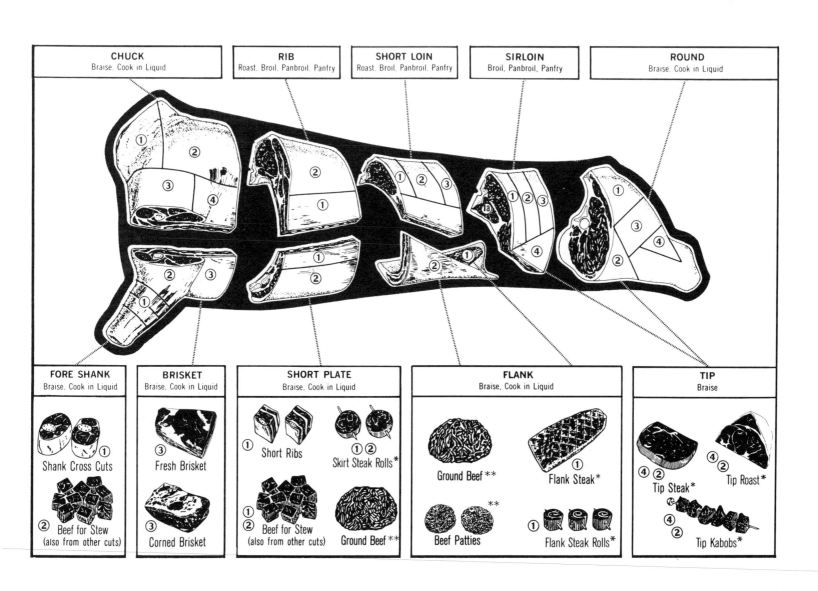

CHUCK
Braise, Cook in Liquid

RIB
Roast, Broil, Panbroil, Panfry

SHORT LOIN
Roast, Broil, Panbroil, Panfry

SIRLOIN
Broil, Panbroil, Panfry

ROUND
Braise, Cook in Liquid

FORE SHANK
Braise, Cook in Liquid

① Shank Cross Cuts

② Beef for Stew
(also from other cuts)

BRISKET
Braise, Cook in Liquid

③ Fresh Brisket

③ Corned Brisket

SHORT PLATE
Braise, Cook in Liquid

① Short Ribs

①② Skirt Steak Rolls*

①② Beef for Stew
(also from other cuts)

Ground Beef**

FLANK
Braise, Cook in Liquid

Ground Beef**

① Flank Steak*

Beef Patties

① Flank Steak Rolls*

TIP
Braise

④② Tip Steak*

④② Tip Roast*

④② Tip Kabobs*

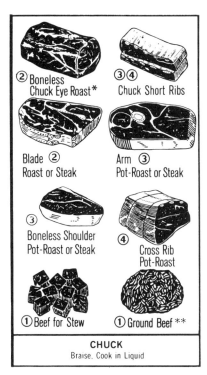

② Boneless Chuck Eye Roast*

③④ Chuck Short Ribs

② Blade Roast or Steak

③ Arm Pot-Roast or Steak

③ Boneless Shoulder Pot-Roast or Steak

④ Cross Rib Pot-Roast

① Beef for Stew

① Ground Beef **

CHUCK
Braise, Cook in Liquid

② Rib Roast

② Rib Steak

② Rib Steak, Boneless

←② ②

Rib Eye (Delmonico) Roast or Steak

RIB
Roast, Broil, Panbroil, Panfry

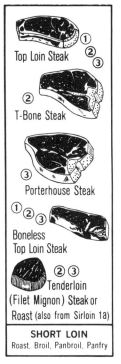

① Top Loin Steak

②③

② T-Bone Steak

③ Porterhouse Steak

①②③ Boneless Top Loin Steak

②③ Tenderloin (Filet Mignon) Steak or Roast (also from Sirloin 1a)

SHORT LOIN
Roast, Broil, Panbroil, Panfry

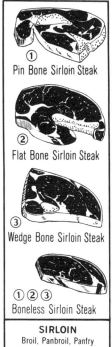

① Pin Bone Sirloin Steak

② Flat Bone Sirloin Steak

③ Wedge Bone Sirloin Steak

①②③ Boneless Sirloin Steak

SIRLOIN
Broil, Panbroil, Panfry

③ Round Steak

④ Heel of Round

③ Top Round Steak*

① Boneless Rump Roast (Rolled)*

③ Bottom Round Roast or Steak*

③ Cubed Steak*

③ Eye of Round*

Ground Beef **

ROUND
Braise, Cook in Liquid

Cuts of beef/27

Beef varies in quality more than any other meat, so there are more *quality grades:*

 PRIME Tender, flavorful, juicy, with abundant marbling. Much fat, too wasteful for consumer use. Usually sold to fine restaurants, hotels. Not found in supermarkets.

 CHOICE Tender, juicy, moderate marbling. Preferred by most people because there is less fat than prime.

 GOOD More lean than the higher grades. Fairly tender, not as juicy and flavorful because there is less marbling and little fat. Sometimes sold under a house brand-name. This grade pleases a thrifty consumer.

 STANDARD Lean with mild flavor, fairly tender, little marbling, lacks juiciness. Available, but only in a few markets; much less expensive.

 COMMERCIAL From older cattle. Full rich flavor, lacks tenderness. Used mostly for sausage and ground beef.
UTILITY, CUTTER, and **CANNER** From older cattle, not tender or juicy. Used for sausage, ground beef, and related products.

Remember, the store is not required to put the grade on the label. So ask the butcher what you are buying.

Full-cut round steak is one of the most economical and versatile cuts of meat—it is actually three steaks in one: top round, eye round, and bottom round. The top round steak is a flavorful, fairly tender piece of meat that can be fried, sliced for stroganoff, marinated, and used in many different recipes. The eye steak is a small, round piece of meat, which also can be used in a variety of dishes. The bottom round is less tender, and is used mostly as Swiss steak.

I'll show you how much you can save by buying the full-cut round.

Top round steak

Eye round steak

Bottom round steak

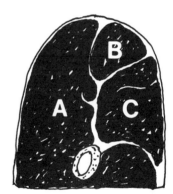

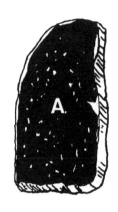

YOUR WAY You buy two slices of top round steak, enough for one meal for your family

2 lbs. at $3.59 per lb. = $ 7.18

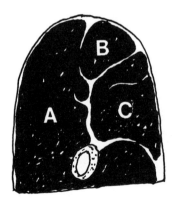

MY WAY I buy two full-cut round steaks, about 4 pounds. I separate the steak into three parts. The top round (2 pounds) is used as dinner steaks. I put the two eye steaks and the two Swiss steaks (bottom round) in the freezer. The dinner comes out to:

2 lbs. at $2.79 per lb. = $5.58.

You paid $7.18 for one meal
I paid $5.58
SAVINGS $1.60 per meal
            $ .80 per pound

And, in addition, I put meat in the freezer.

ROUND STEAK, STUFFED AND BAKED

Take a thin-cut top round steak and stuff with:

chopped celery	1 raw egg
chopped onion	fresh garlic, minced
sour dough French bread, cubed	pinch oregano
	salt and pepper

Spread the stuffing on top of the round steak, roll up, tie strings around it—one inch apart, and bake in the oven at 325 degrees for about one hour.

TIP The best months to buy beef are January through April. Always buy steaks for the freezer in the winter. In summer everyone wants to barbecue, and high demand means high prices. By the same rule, buy soup meat and bones in the summer, when nobody wants to slave over a hot stove. Know the price of the various cuts and buy them when they're on sale.

When you buy a full-cut steak, make sure that a piece of the top round was not cut out before you bought it.

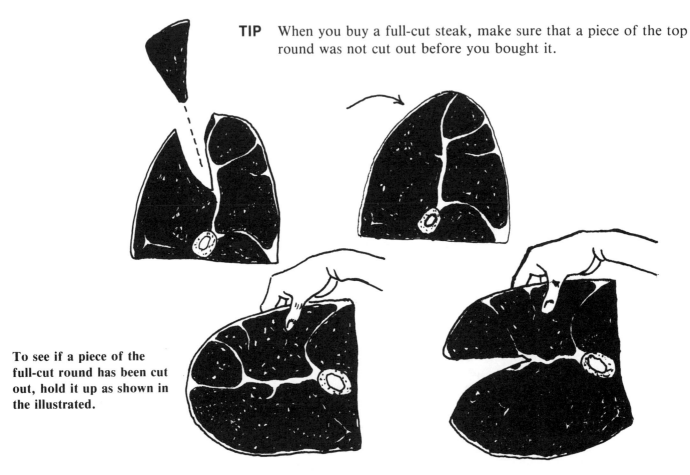

To see if a piece of the full-cut round has been cut out, hold it up as shown in the illustrated.

Compare the two pictures to see what happens.

YOUR WAY You buy two eye round steaks, about one pound total weight.

$$1 \text{ lb. at } \$3.89 \text{ per lb.} = \$3.89$$

MY WAY I buy two full-cut round steaks and separate them into the eye steaks, Swiss steaks, and top round. I use the eye steaks and freeze the Swiss and top round steaks.

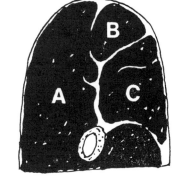

$$1 \text{ lb. full-cut round at } \$2.79 \text{ per lb.} = \$2.79$$
SAVINGS $1.10 per lb.

TIP Always watch for sales because round steaks are often on sale and you can make so much with them.

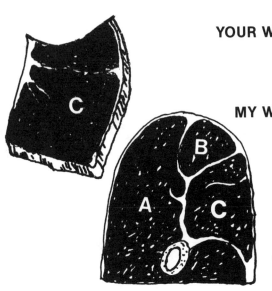

YOUR WAY You want Swiss steak for dinner, so you buy two slices of bottom round steak, about 1½ pounds.

1½ lbs. at $2.88 per lb. = $4.32

MY WAY I use the bottom round from two full-cut round steaks.

1½ lbs. full-cut round at $2.79 per lb. = $4.19

SAVINGS $0.13 per meal
$0.09 per pound

(Not much, but the savings add up!)

TIP You can use several cuts of meat for Swiss steak: chuck steak, bottom round, rump roast, even cross-rib roast. Check prices and buy whichever cut is cheapest.

This is how much you can save by buying a full-cut round:

YOUR WAY

2 lbs. top round at $3.59 per lb. = $ 7.18
1½ lbs. bottom round at $2.88 per lb. = $ 4.32
½ lb. eye of round at $3.89 per lb. = $ 1.95
Total = $13.45

MY WAY

4 lbs. full-cut round at $2.79 per lb. = $11.16
SAVINGS $ 2.29

Try this recipe sent in by one of my radio listeners:

QUICK ORIENTAL DISH

(Tonalyn Case, Dublin, California)

1 lb.	round steak	½	green pepper	
½ cup	soy sauce	½ lb.	green beans or snow	
1 tsp.	pepper		peas	
1 tsp.	garlic salt	¼ cup	water	
1 tsp.	mustard powder	6 Tbsp.	vegetable oil	
1	small onion	2 cups	cooked rice	
½ lb.	mushrooms			

Slice beef in thin strips. In bowl, mix first five ingredients, set aside. Slice vegetables. In large frying pan, add half the oil and saute meat until just brown. Put beef back into bowl. (Don't overcook: have the pan super hot and fry quickly). Add the rest of oil to pan and saute the onion and green peppers. Add green beans (or snow peas), then sliced mushrooms. Saute vegetables until they are bright in color. Add water; cover and cook 2 minutes. Add beef and stir. Pour over rice. *4 servings*.

"Never buy tenderized steaks."

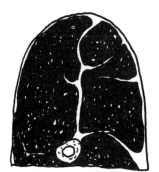

YOUR WAY   You buy a full-cut round steak, tenderized.

> 1 lb. tenderized round at $3.19 per lb. = $3.19

MY WAY   I buy a full-cut round, not tenderized. I ask the butcher to put it through the tenderizer machine (no extra charge), or I do it myself at home by scoring both sides horizontally and vertically.

> 1 lb. untenderized round at $2.79 per lb. = $2.79
> **SAVINGS** $0.40 per lb.

You pay $0.40 more per pound because the steak was tenderized. This doesn't really make sense, but most supermarkets charge more for tenderized steaks.

TIP   *Chicken-fry steak* is nothing more than bottom-round steak. Buy full-cut round and do it yourself.

YOUR WAY You want a pot roast and an oven roast. You buy a bottom round roast and a sirloin tip roast, about 3 pounds each.

> 3 lb. bottom round roast at $2.88 per lb. = $ 8.64
> 3 lb. sirloin tip roast at $2.99 per lb. = $ 8.97
> Total = $17.61

Bottom round roast   **Sirloin tip roast**

MY WAY I have a full-cut round steak cut specially, four inches thick, weighing about 6 pounds. When I get home, I simply cut it across the middle. I get an oven roast from the top piece (top round makes a delicious roast—as good as sirloin tip) and a pot roast from the bottom piece.

> 6 lb. full-cut round at $2.79 per lb. = $16.74
> **SAVINGS** $ 0.87

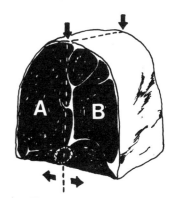

A - Top round roast

B - Bottom round roast

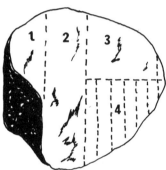

1 & 2 - London broils

3 - Top round roast

4 - Top round steaks

YOUR WAY You buy a London broil—which is actually the first cuts from a boneless top round—and pay a high price to get it.

4 lbs. at $3.79 per lb. = $15.16

MY WAY I ask the butcher for a whole boneless top round—about 12 pounds. (I may have to give the butcher some advance notice.) This may seem like a large piece of meat, but I'll get a lot of meals out of it. I ask him to cut a small and a large London broil—the first cuts—each about three inches thick. I'll get about 4 pounds of London broil. The rest could be cut into thinner top round steaks or split in half to make two roasts. Have the butcher remove the last three inches—the tapered end of the roast, trim off the fat, and grind for hamburger or cut into stew meat.

4 lbs. London broil at $3.79 per lb. = $15.16
4 lbs. top round at $3.59 per lb. = $14.36
SAVINGS $ .20 per lb.

And I put several round steaks and two roasts in the freezer.

TIP You don't often see top round roasts in the supermarket counters because the butcher makes more money cutting and selling them as steaks. Ask your butcher to split a whole top round into two roasts, each about 5 or 6 pounds. They make a very lovely oven roast, with great flavor.

YOUR WAY You buy a sirloin tip roast, wrapped and ready to go.

MY WAY I buy a sirloin tip roast. I ask the butcher for the "solid" side. The "soft" side of the sirloin tip is not a solid piece of meat. It will fall apart when I try to carve it.

"Soft" and "solid" are terms only the butcher knows, but you are way ahead of the game if you know them too. You always get the soft side unless you specifically ask for the solid because the butcher makes more money cutting the solid side into steaks.

TIP Did you know that the sirloin tip is not from the loin of beef but from the round? Actually the sirloin tip is a highly overrated roast. A cross-rib roast is more tender and flavorful, and usually costs about $0.20 per pound less.

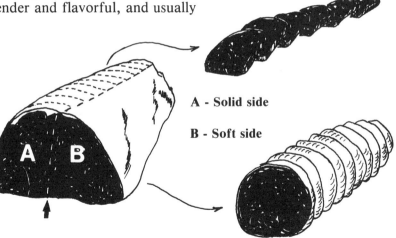

A - Solid side

B - Soft side

Beef—sirloin tip roast / 39

"Don't buy sirloin tip steaks; buy a sirloin tip roast."

YOUR WAY

Most butchers cut sirloin tip steaks and 6-pound roasts from a whole sirloin tip roast. The whole sirloin roast weighs about 12 pounds and is split into the "solid" side and "soft" side. The 6-pound solid side is cut into sirloin tip steaks. The soft side is packaged as a 6-pound roast. That's what you get when you buy from the counter.

MY WAY

I buy the entire boneless sirloin tip roast, which always sells for less per pound than the soft-side roast. I ask the butcher to cut a coulotte steak from the top. This is my idea—most butchers don't do this. After the coulotte is removed, I ask him to remove the "rough" portion from the soft side and split the roast in two parts, solid and soft. When I get home I cut sirloin tip steaks from the solid side (the end piece can be a cube steak), and roll the soft side in a *jet net* (ask the butcher to give you one) or tie strings around it to make it into a roast. Here's what I save:

2 lbs. coulotte steak at $3.89 = $ 7.78
5 lbs. sirloin tip steaks at $3.59 = $17.95
5 lbs. soft-side roast at $2.99 = $14.95
Total $40.68
12 lbs. sirloin tip roast at $2.79 = $33.48
SAVINGS $ 7.20

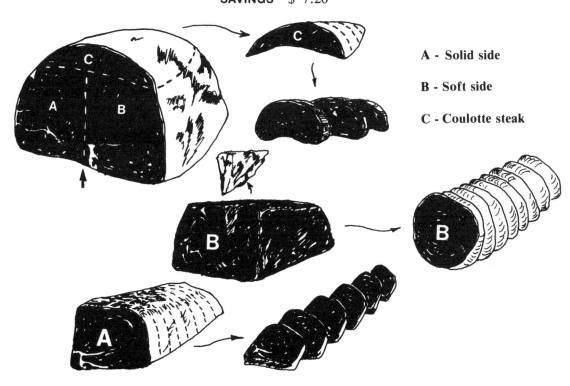

A - Solid side

B - Soft side

C - Coulotte steak

YOUR WAY You buy a sirloin tip steak, regular thickness. If you buy it cut thin, you probably pay more.

1 lb. sirloin tip steak at $3.59 per lb. = $3.59

MY WAY I ask the butcher for the "solid" side sirloin tip roast, which I cut into steaks myself. Each 1-pound steak costs me: $2.99.

SAVINGS $0.60 per lb.

TIP Always cut a steak at least one-inch thick when you plan to broil or barbecue it. A thinner steak will lose a lot of juice and turn out dry.

YOUR WAY You buy a package of sliced steak for stroganoff or sukiyaki. It is all cut up and ready to go.

1 lb. sliced steak at $3.89 per lb. = $3.89

MY WAY I buy a full-cut round steak and cut it into strips myself. In some markets the butcher will do this for you. I could also use a small sirloin tip roast, a small cross-rib roast, or a flank steak, depending on the price. I look for sales and pick the cut that is the cheapest.

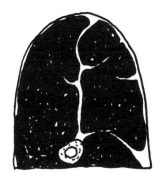

1 lb. full-cut round steak at $2.79 per lb. = $2.79
SAVINGS $1.10 per lb.

TIP It's easier to do your slicing if you have an electric meat slicer, but if you don't, here's what to do. Put the meat in your freezer for about an hour or so—longer if necessary—until it becomes firm but not frozen. Then it will slice easily.

"Never buy what you can make yourself for less."

YOUR WAY You buy cube steaks, tenderized and packaged.

1 lb. cube steaks at $3.79 per lb. = $3.79

MY WAY I never buy prepared cube steaks because I can make my own for so much less. I buy a full-cut round steak *or* a cross-rib roast or steak, sirloin tip roast or steak, top round steak, Jewish fillet, or flat-iron steak—even chuck steak if it is very well aged (ask your butcher).

All I do is score the steak horizontally and vertically on both sides with a paring knife. If the steak is too thick, I place between wax paper and pound it thin before scoring.

1 lb. round steak at $2.79 per lb. = $2.79
SAVINGS $1.00 per lb.

TIP The wax paper keeps the meat from sticking to the mallet, but sometimes the paper disintegrates. Try this trick: instead of wax paper, use plastic produce bags. They won't fall apart, and you get them *free* at the supermarket.

YOUR WAY You buy a nice thick chateaubriand for a special dinner.

MY WAY I buy a top sirloin and ask the butcher to cut it two inches thick. Chateaubriand (a French word meaning "silver castle") is technically a piece from the fillet, but today most shops sell top sirloin as chateaubriand, and the butcher may charge you more for the fancy name.

TIP Many butchers now cut only boneless top sirloin steaks because they can take out the piece of fillet and sell it for a higher price. But when you buy a sirloin steak with the bone in it, you get the most for your money with a round-bone sirloin. Never buy a pin-bone or flat-bone sirloin—there's too much waste.

 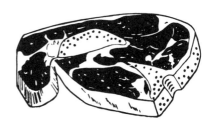 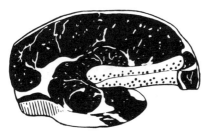

Round-bone sirloin steak   **Pin-bone sirloin steak**   **Flat-bone sirloin steak**

YOUR WAY You want to make shish kabobs for company, so you buy a package of shish kabobs.

2 lbs. shish kabobs at $3.98 per lb. = $7.96

MY WAY I buy a top sirloin steak, remove the fat, cube the steak myself (an easy job), and it's ready for the skewers.

2 lbs. top sirloin at $3.89 per lb. = $7.78
SAVINGS $0.20 for the meal.

Every little bit helps, and you get the size cubes you want!

YOUR WAY   You buy two T-bone steaks to barbecue for dinner.

T-bone steak

MY WAY   I buy two porterhouse steaks, picking the ones with the largest fillets (the tenderloin).

Porterhouse steak

Porterhouse and T-bone are usually the same price. But even if the porterhouse is 10 cents a pound more, it's a better buy because you get a fillet that would sell for almost $6.00 per pound. The T-bone has little or no fillet.

"A porterhouse steak is two steaks in one."

YOUR WAY You buy two New York (or top loin) steaks.

2 lbs. New York steak at $4.98 per lb. = $9.96

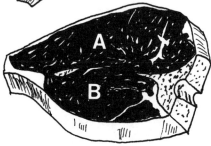

MY WAY I buy two porterhouse steaks, about 2 pounds each. When I get home, I remove the bones—a very easy job—and save the bones (about half a pound) for soup. The top part of the porterhouse is the *New York* or *top loin steak*. The bottom part is a *fillet steak*. So I separate the porterhouse steaks and end up with two New Yorks, plus two fillets that are worth $5.49 a pound when cut separately.

A - New York or top loin steak

B - Fillet steak

2 lbs. porterhouse at $3.89 per lb. = $7.78
SAVINGS $2.18

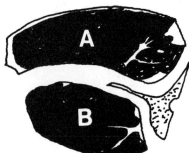

Here's my total savings when I buy porterhouse instead of New York and fillet:

2 lbs. New York at $4.98 per lb. = $ 9.96
1½ lbs. of fillet (½ lb. bone) at $5.49 per lb. = $ 8.24
Total $18.20
4 lbs. porterhouse at $3.89 per lb. = $15.96
SAVINGS $ 2.24

Even paying for the bone I am ahead.

"Why pay extra money for the butcher to remove a bone?"

TIP In California the top loin steak is called a "New York" steak! In the Midwest it's called "top loin," and in some other parts of the country a "strip steak."

YOUR WAY You buy a thick fillet for Beef Wellington. It costs a fortune.

1¾ lbs. fillet at $5.59 per lb. = $9.79

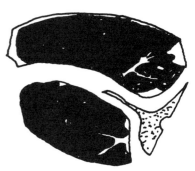

MY WAY I ask the butcher to cut me a 2-pound porterhouse steak. I take it home and remove the bone. The bone weighs about ¼ pound and I save it for soup. I separate the meat and end up with a 1-pound New York steak and a ¾-pound fillet. I wrap the two steaks in pastry dough and bake separately. Delicious Wellington, and I still have some money in my pocket!

2 lb. porterhouse at $3.89 per lb. = $7.78
SAVINGS $2.01

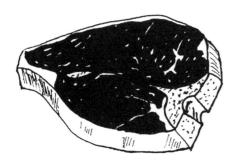

TIP When you buy a porterhouse steak, watch the trim. Here is a porterhouse, perfectly trimmed:

Here are examples of a poor trim—a clod of fat near the fillet, and a long, long tail. Also watch for a large edge of fat.

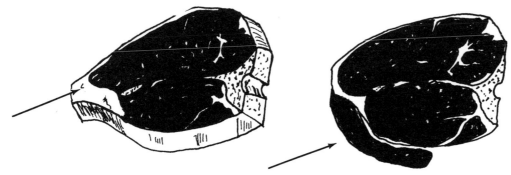

Sometimes meat on sale is not trimmed properly. You may pay less per pound for the steak, but after you throw away the fat, bones, and excessive tail, you end up paying more.

Aging Meat

TIP For a really special steak or roast, ask your butcher to age the meat.

Markets do not age meat—it comes in today and goes out tomorrow. When meat ages it shrinks, weighs less, and the butcher takes a loss. Shops that do age meat charge more, but you get very good flavor.

So for a really special occasion, ask your butcher if he'll hang the meat for you—14 days for beef, 7 days for lamb. Have him weigh the roast. You pay for it, then keep the receipt and tell him when you'll be back to pick it up.

Expect to lose about 1 to 1½ pounds for an 8-pound roast for shrinkage and trimming the outside. But the meat will have developed outstanding flavor, and you'll be able to cut it with your fork.

Caution: Don't try this at home because success depends on the meat and bone being trimmed properly after aging. It's hard to do this without a butcher's equipment.

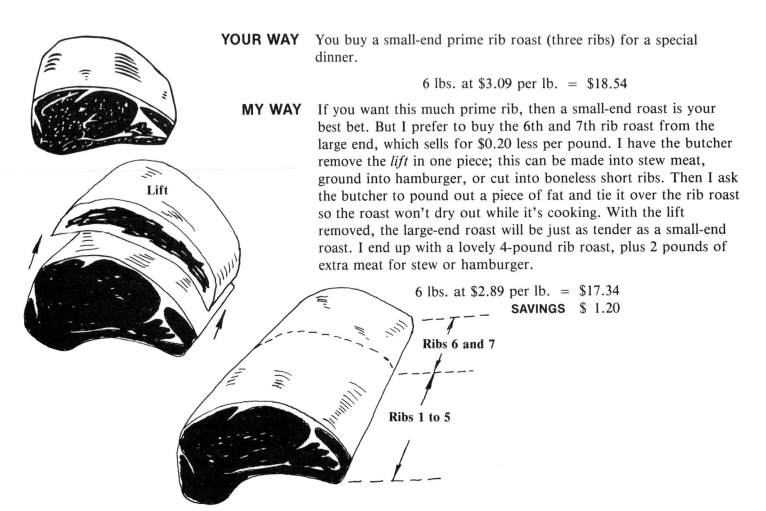

YOUR WAY You buy a small-end prime rib roast (three ribs) for a special dinner.

6 lbs. at $3.09 per lb. = $18.54

MY WAY If you want this much prime rib, then a small-end roast is your best bet. But I prefer to buy the 6th and 7th rib roast from the large end, which sells for $0.20 less per pound. I have the butcher remove the *lift* in one piece; this can be made into stew meat, ground into hamburger, or cut into boneless short ribs. Then I ask the butcher to pound out a piece of fat and tie it over the rib roast so the roast won't dry out while it's cooking. With the lift removed, the large-end roast will be just as tender as a small-end roast. I end up with a lovely 4-pound rib roast, plus 2 pounds of extra meat for stew or hamburger.

6 lbs. at $2.89 per lb. = $17.34
SAVINGS $ 1.20

Lift

Ribs 6 and 7

Ribs 1 to 5

TIP If you like a boneless roast, ask the butcher to remove the rib roast bones all in one piece and tie it to the roast with a string. While cooking, the bones will flavor the meat. When it comes out of the oven, cut the strings and remove the bones. The roast will be as easy to carve as a loaf of bread.

YOUR WAY You buy rib eye steaks—or perhaps in your market they call them market steaks, spencer steaks, or Delmonico steaks (more of those made-up names).

2 lbs. market steaks at $4.59 per lb. = $9.18

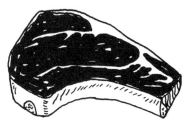

MY WAY I buy a rib steak and take the bone out myself. It's easy to do and requires no special skill. When the butcher takes the bone out of a rib steak, it becomes a rib eye steak and the price changes. This is known in the trade as paying for labor, service, and convenience.

2 lbs. rib steak at $3.59 per lb. = $7.18
SAVINGS $1.00 per lb.

Even with the soup bone I'm ahead of the game.

TIP Don't buy the larger rib steaks, because they have a lift on them and consequently are not as tender. Some markets also sell a "boneless rib steak," which is from the large end. It sells for less per pound but has a lift on it. It's not a good buy.

Poor buy　　　　　　　　**Good buy**

TIP An even better way to save on market steaks and have some meat for the freezer is to buy the 6th and 7th rib roast and have the butcher remove the lift and cut it into stew meat. The rest of the roast can then be cut into market steaks. Make sure they are at least an inch thick. The bones make delicious beef spareribs.

From a 5 lb. rib roast at $2.89 per lb. and costing $14.45, I get:

3 lbs. market steaks at $4.59 per lb. =	$13.77
1 lb. beef stew at $2.89 per lb. =	$ 2.89
1 lb. beef spareribs at $0.98 per lb. =	$ 0.98
Total	$17.64
SAVINGS	$3.19

TIP What is a skirt steak? It is a long, narrow piece of meat, about 4 inches wide and 20 inches long, that lies on the back side of the prime rib roast. It is almost a forgotten cut, yet it has a lovely flavor. If you've never tried one, I'm sure you'll love it. It is quite economical—no bone, fat, or waste.

If you make your own Chinese dishes, try the skirt steak. Slice into strips on a 45-degree angle, about 1/16-inch thick. You can use it in any recipe that calls for flank steak, but it cooks very well in a stir-fry. Skirt is a lot cheaper per pound and has excellent flavor and tenderness.

Skirt steak rolls

"Don't buy steaks; cut them from roasts."

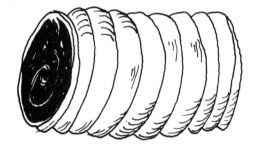

YOUR WAY You buy four cross-rib steaks (sometimes called "barbecue steaks") about ¾ lb. each.

3 lbs. cross-rib steaks at $3.09 per lb. = $9.27

MY WAY I buy a 3-pound cross-rib roast at about $2.79 per lb. When I get home, I cut it into four steaks (¾ lb. each). It's a simple cutting job because the roast is boneless. I save money because I don't pay for labor and service.

Each steak cost you $2.30
Each steak cost me $2.10
SAVING $0.20 per steak

TIP As a rule, steaks are about $0.15 to $0.20 per pound more than roasts. Buy a roast and cut it yourself—or ask the butcher to cut it and you will still pay the lower price.

TIP When you buy a cross-rib roast, always buy the center cut. Don't get the end cut—the one that comes to a point—because the slices are not uniform. (The drawing shows what I'm talking about.)

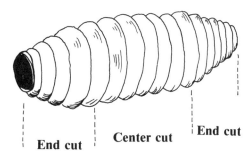

End cut   **Center cut**   **End cut**

The cross-rib roast is every bit as good as a sirloin tip roast. Why pay $0.20 a pound more for the sirloin tip?

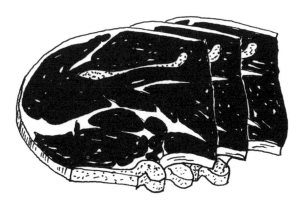

YOUR WAY You buy three chuck steaks, about 1½ lbs. each.

4½ lbs. chuck steaks at $1.68 per lb. = $7.56

MY WAY I buy a 4½ lb. blade chuck roast and have the butcher cut it into three steaks. (Don't try to do this at home!)

Each steak cost you $2.52 ($1.68 per lb.)
Each steak cost me $2.22 ($1.48 per lb.)
SAVINGS $0.30 per steak

TIP You can marinate a chuck steak (overnight, for best results) and broil or barbecue it just like a sirloin steak. Make sure that the marinade contains wine or vinegar to tenderize the meat.

58/Save on beef

MARINADES FOR BLADE STEAK

1	blade steak, cut 1 inch thick
¼ cup	wine vinegar
3 Tbsp.	soy sauce
2 Tbsp.	oil
2 Tbsp.	catsup
1 clove	garlic, minced

Pour marinade over steak. Cover and marinate in refrigerator 6 hours or overnight, turning at least once. Broil or barbecue to desired doneness.

BEER MARINADE

1 cup	beer
2 cloves	garlic, smashed
	juice of one lemon
1 tsp.	oregano
	salt and pepper

Or create your own marinade, using wine, onions, fresh ginger, honey, and your favorite spices.

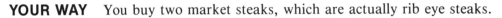

YOUR WAY You buy two market steaks, which are actually rib eye steaks.

1½ lbs. rib eye steaks at $4.59 per lb. = $6.89

MY WAY I buy a first-cut blade chuck roast that weighs about 4 pounds. The first cut of a blade chuck is next to the prime rib roast and contains some rib eye steak. When I get home I remove all the bone, which is very easy.

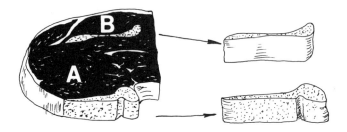

I cut the top pieces of meat into stew meat or ground chuck. The bottom piece is the rib eye, and from that I make market steaks. The bones go into the freezer for soup and I feed the fat to the birds. For all this I pay just $5.92 (4 lbs. at $1.48).

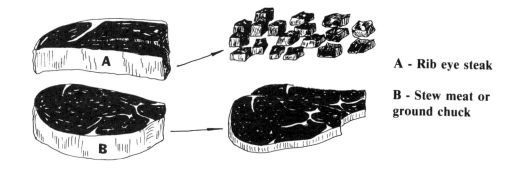

A - Rib eye steak

B - Stew meat or ground chuck

1½ lbs. rib eye from blade chuck at $1.48 per lb. = $2.22
SAVINGS $4.67 or $3.11 per lb.

I save about as much as I spend when I buy a blade chuck:

1½ lbs. of stew meat or ground chuck at $2.89 = $ 4.34
1½ lbs. of rib eye steaks at $4.59 = $ 6.88
Total $11.22
Blade chuck $ 5.92
TOTAL SAVINGS $ 5.30

"What is a Jewish fillet and what is a flat-iron steak?"

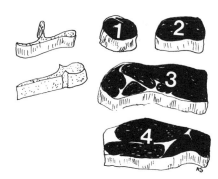

TIP Above the bone in the center-cut and the seven-bone chuck roast are two pieces of meat that, if sold separately, would go for premium prices. You can save by buying the roasts, boning them, and separating the meat into:

1. the "Jewish fillet," a small, round piece of meat that can be made into cube steaks or a tender pot roast;

2. the "flat-iron" steak or "fluff steak" (more of those made-up names), which is tender enough to be broiled or fried, or used any way you want;

3. and 4. two large pieces of chuck for pot roast, stew meat, or ground chuck.

The Jewish fillet sells for about $2.50 per pound; the flat-iron sells for about $3.50. So you'll save about $1 to $2 per pound by buying a seven-bone roast instead.

TIP When you buy a seven-bone chuck roast, be sure a piece hasn't been removed (see drawing). You're paying for a whole roast—be sure you get it!

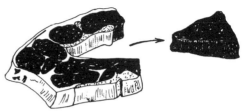

YOUR WAY You buy a package of short ribs. They are nice and lean, but when you cook them they turn out to be tough.

Short ribs from the prime rib roast

MY WAY There are two kinds of short ribs: *short ribs* from the prime rib roast are loaded with marbling, so they are tender and flavorful. *Chuck short ribs* (sometimes *triangle* short ribs) are very lean and good, but they have to be cooked a long time to be tender because they have little or no marbling. Both kinds are about the same price, but you should know the best to be buying.

Chuck short ribs (triangle ribs)

YOUR WAY

You buy packaged stew meat already cut up. The package doesn't say that the meat is not from one cut, but scraps collected by the butcher— a piece from here and a piece from there. Some are well marbled and tender, others are tough and dry. And the meat was cut several days before.

3 lbs. stew meat at $2.89 per lb. = $8.67

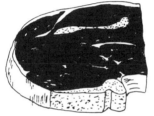

MY WAY

I buy either a blade chuck roast or a seven-bone chuck roast, about 4 pounds. If I buy the blade chuck, I ask the butcher to bone it out, or do it myself. I save the bones for soup, the fat for the birds, and cut up the meat for stew. Or I cut the top portion (the section with the skin and grade marks) into stew meat and make two steaks from the bottom portion (see page 61).

A seven-bone chuck roast yields more stew but costs a little more per pound than the blade. I use the top portion for cube steaks, or cut it all into stew meat (see page 62).

4 lbs. blade chuck at $1.48 per lb. = $5.92
SAVINGS $2.75, or $1.41 per lb.

Even with the fat and bone (about 1 pound), I am still ahead.

JERKY

(Jerky is a delicious snack, but expensive. You can save by making your own, using fresh beef brisket—try to get it on sale.)

Partially freeze meat before slicing, to make it easier to cut. Cut into thin strips, about ½ inch wide and as long as you can. Place the meat in a plastic container and cover with:

⅓ cup	liquid smoke	2 tsp.	cayenne pepper
½ cup	sugar		(optional—for hot
½ cup	salt		flavor)
2 qts.	water		

Marinate meat for 2 full days in cool place (you do not have to refrigerate). Remove meat and pat dry. Place on cookie sheet; separate so pieces do not touch. Bake in 300 degree oven for 1 hour. Remove and cool. Store in a jar; do not refrigerate.

YOUR WAY   You want to make beef soup, so you buy 3 pounds of beef shanks.

3 lbs. beef shanks at $1.49 per lb. = $4.47

MY WAY   I buy 3 pounds of beef neck bones. They are loaded with meat and are much less expensive than shanks.

3 lbs. neck bones at $0.79 per lb. = $2.37
SAVINGS $2.10, or $0.70 per lb.

TIP   Oxtails are tasty and economical. Sometimes you'll see them in the counter, but you may have to order them in advance. Try them braised or in a soup.

MINESTRONE

(This recipe is from my friend Art Hill, Petaluma, California. Art was a chef for over 50 years. He tried many recipes for minestrone and finally settled on this one. It is out of this world! It will serve 16 people one cup each. Freeze the leftovers for future use.)

To prepare the stock:

Fill a large pot with 5 quarts of water. Add the following ingredients:

2½ lbs.	marrow bones	1	small onion, chopped
2 lbs.	beef neck bones	2	celery sprig tops
1	carrot, chopped		

Simmer slowly for 4 hours (5, if you have the time). Now strain to get clear broth.

In a frying pan, saute the following ingredients:

½ lb.	salt pork, diced	1 cup	kidney beans
2	large leeks, diced	1	small sprig fresh rosemary
2 cups	diced onion		
½ cup	diced carrot	1 pinch	oregano
½ cup	diced celery	3	large garlic cloves
1 cup	diced tomato		

Add sauteed ingredients to the stock. Simmer uncovered for one more hour. For the last 20 minutes, throw in 1 cup of pasta. Add salt and pepper to taste. Serve with grated parmesan cheese and some good French bread.

"Do a grease test on your hamburger."

TIP Ground beef is the most popular item in the meat department. Butchers won't tell you this, but the law states that a butcher is allowed to put up to 30 percent fat in regular ground beef. So you automatically lose four to five ounces. In extra lean ground beef butchers are allowed up to 22 percent fat.

Look at it this way:

> 1 lb. of ground beef at $1.49 per lb. = $1.49
> The fat runoff (five ounces) is $0.47 worth of that.
> Your real cost is $1.96 for a full pound of cooked meat.

For extra lean at $2.39 per lb. and 22 percent fat, you lose 3½ ounces, or $0.52 worth. So you are actually paying $2.91 per lb.

Make a grease test for yourself and really see what you are getting for your money. Buy a pound of ground beef, cook it, and pour the grease into a measuring cup.

Now buy a blade chuck roast. Bone it and grind it yourself, or ask the butcher to do it. Cook it and pour the grease into a measuring cup, and compare. Taste the difference between the packaged and fresh-ground hamburger. You will never buy packaged hamburger again!

GROUND CHUCK AND SPINACH

(In San Francisco they call this a ''Joe's Special.'')

1 lb.	ground chuck	onions (to taste)
1 pkg.	frozen leaf spinach or large bunch fresh spinach	garlic (to taste) parsley salt and pepper
2	eggs	1 fresh lemon
olive oil		parmesan cheese

Cook spinach in sauce-pan; then drain well. In frying pan brown onions, garlic, and parsley in olive oil. Remove from pan. Brown ground chuck; drain off grease. Return onions, garlic and parsley to the pan. Mix in spinach and eggs. Cook 'til eggs are firm. Squeeze the juice of the lemon on top and sprinkle with cheese.

STUFFED HAMBURGERS

Take two hamburger patties; make a cavity in each. Stuff with chopped onions, garlic, parsley, mushrooms, and canned chili peppers. Create your own combination of ingredients! Press the two patties together, squeeze the edges to seal in the stuffing, add salt and pepper to taste, and broil, fry, or barbecue. My wife Dee makes this for me, and believe me, it's delicious.

"Grind your own meat and you'll never buy ground meat again!"

YOUR WAY You buy a package of ground chuck. You don't know that only some of it is actually chuck; the butcher also puts in all kinds of lean scraps.

3 lbs. ground chuck at $2.39 per lb. = $7.17

MY WAY I buy a 4-pound blade chuck roast, which are often on sale. I can ask the butcher to bone and grind it, but for the best results I grind the meat myself at home. The big grinders in the butcher shop need about 2 to 3 pounds of prime in order to push out the meat, so some of this prime gets mixed into your chuck.

I grind the whole roast if I want 3 pounds of hamburger (there will be about a pound of fat and bones). Or I can grind the top part and cut the lower part into market steaks, getting 1½ pounds ground meat and 1½ pounds market steaks.

4 lbs. blade chuck at $1.48 per lb. = $5.92
SAVINGS $1.25

MEAL-IN-ONE

(This recipe was sent in by one of my radio listeners, Mrs. R. L. Cooper of Walnut Creek, California.)

Cook the following ingredients in a frying pan:

1 lb.	ground beef, crumbled	½ tsp.	paprika
¼ cup	orange, lime, or lemon juice (or vinegar)	1 tsp.	Worcestershire sauce
			salt and pepper to taste

Drain off juice and set aside.

3-4 cups	cabbage, shredded	2 Tbsp.	juice (orange or whatever)
2-3	apples, pared and sliced		shredded cheese

In a well-buttered casserole, layer cabbage and sliced apples, salting each layer. Place ground beef on top and pour juice over top. Shred your favorite cheese over top. Cover and bake for 40 minutes.

TIP Use a full-cut round steak to make ground round.

Now you're ready to buy beef "My Way." Remember to:

- Know the names and prices of the various cuts.
- Watch for sales, especially on full-cut round steak and blade chuck—your best buys.
- Don't pay extra for tenderized steaks and cube steaks; do it yourself.
- Try a little cutting at home: make steaks from roasts, slice your own steak for stroganoff, cut your own cubes for kabobs and stew, and bone your own rib eye steaks.
- Grind your own beef, you'll save money and get better tasting hamburger.

The prices of beef will change, but the system will always work. Believe me, your bill at the grocery store will be less.

LAMB

Lamb is produced from young animals, usually less than a year old, so the meat is tender and delicately flavored. The quality does not vary as much as it does with beef. The USDA grades lamb Prime, Choice, Good, Standard and Commercial—but at the retail level you'll see mostly Choice.

You can buy lamb all year round, but the best sales and prices are likely to be in the spring. Although lamb prices are generally high, there are some bargain cuts, and even with the more popular cuts there are plenty of ways to save money.

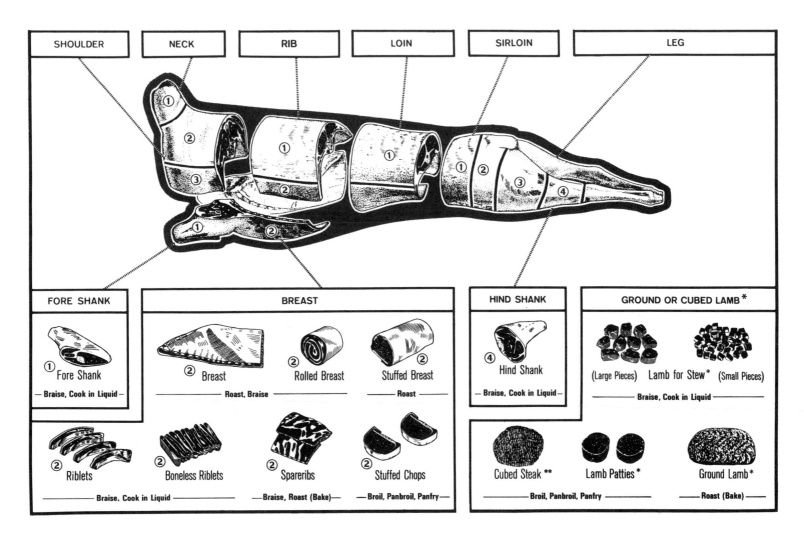

SHOULDER	NECK	RIB	LOIN	SIRLOIN	LEG

FORE SHANK

① Fore Shank

— Braise, Cook in Liquid —

② Riblets

— Braise, Cook in Liquid —

BREAST

② Breast

② Rolled Breast

② Stuffed Breast

— Roast, Braise —

— Roast —

② Boneless Riblets

② Spareribs

② Stuffed Chops

— Braise, Cook in Liquid —

— Braise, Roast (Bake) —

— Broil, Panbroil, Panfry —

HIND SHANK

④ Hind Shank

— Braise, Cook in Liquid —

GROUND OR CUBED LAMB*

(Large Pieces) Lamb for Stew* (Small Pieces)

— Braise, Cook in Liquid —

Cubed Steak **

Lamb Patties *

Ground Lamb*

— Broil, Panbroil, Panfry —

— Roast (Bake) —

74 / Save on lamb

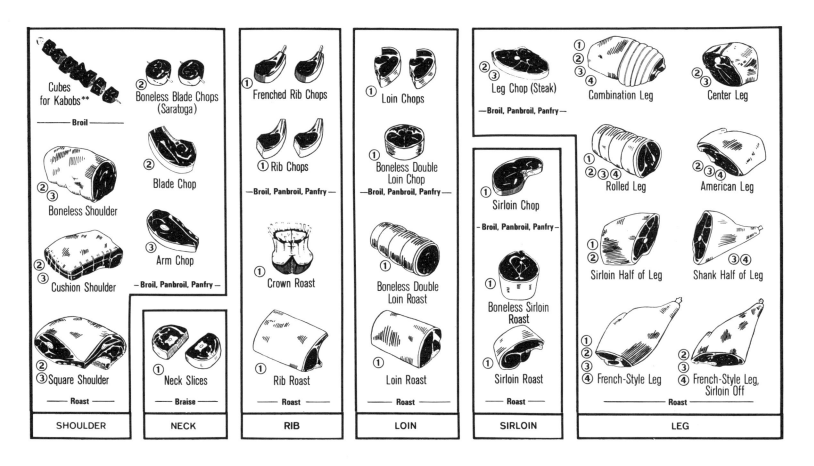

Cubes for Kabobs✶✶

— Broil —

② ③ **Boneless Shoulder**

② ③ **Cushion Shoulder**

② ③ **Square Shoulder**

— Roast —

SHOULDER

② **Boneless Blade Chops (Saratoga)**

② **Blade Chop**

③ **Arm Chop**

— Broil, Panbroil, Panfry —

① **Neck Slices**

— Braise —

NECK

① **Frenched Rib Chops**

① **Rib Chops**

— Broil, Panbroil, Panfry —

① **Crown Roast**

① **Rib Roast**

— Roast —

RIB

① **Loin Chops**

① **Boneless Double Loin Chop**

— Broil, Panbroil, Panfry —

① **Boneless Double Loin Roast**

① **Loin Roast**

— Roast —

LOIN

① **Sirloin Chop**

— Broil, Panbroil, Panfry —

① **Boneless Sirloin Roast**

① **Sirloin Roast**

— Roast —

SIRLOIN

② ③ ④ **Leg Chop (Steak)**

— Broil, Panbroil, Panfry —

① ② ③ ④ **Combination Leg**

① ② ③ ④ **Rolled Leg**

① ② **Sirloin Half of Leg**

① ② ③ ④ **French-Style Leg**

② ③ **Center Leg**

② ③ ④ **American Leg**

③ ④ **Shank Half of Leg**

② ③ ④ **French-Style Leg, Sirloin Off**

— Roast —

LEG

✶ Lamb for stew or grinding may be made from any cut.

✶✶ Kabobs or cube steaks may be made from any thick solid piece of boneless Lamb.

This chart approved by
National Live Stock and Meat Board

Lamb chart / 75

"Even if you only save a few pennies, they add up!"

YOUR WAY You buy half a leg of lamb to roast for a family dinner.

3 lbs. at $2.49 per lb. = $7.47
or $14.94 for two of them.

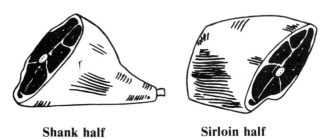

Shank half   **Sirloin half**

MY WAY I buy a whole leg of lamb, which is usually cheaper than a half. I ask the butcher to cut it in half. When I get home, I freeze half for another roast. Or I can have the other half either cut into steaks or cube it for kabobs.

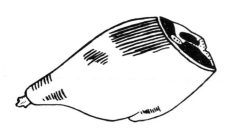

6 lbs. whole leg at $2.39 per lb. = $14.34
SAVINGS $0.10 per lb.

Even if you don't save a lot of money in a purchase like this, you still come out way ahead by having meat in the freezer, which can save you an extra trip to the store—and you know what a convenience *that* can be!

TIP I am occasionally asked if I should skin a leg of lamb. I always say that skinning a leg of lamb lets all the juices out of it, so you end up with a dry roast. If you don't like the skin—or *fell* as the butchers call it—peel it off *after* roasting. Also, it is not necessary to remove the gland from the leg of lamb as was done years ago. The gland does not give the meat a bad flavor, and cutting a hole in the skin will let the juices out.

YOUR WAY You buy lamb steaks to broil on the grill.

3 lbs. at $3.69 per lb. = $11.07

MY WAY I buy a whole leg of lamb (on sale, because they're usually quite expensive) and have the butcher saw it into steaks. I save the shank portion for baking or for a stew.

6 lbs. at $2.39 per lb. = $14.34
SAVINGS $1.30 per lb. or $3.90 for 3 lbs.

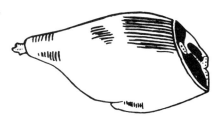

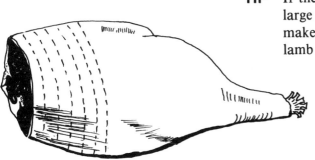

TIP If the butcher will cut it for you, buy the leg of lamb with the large loin chops on it. Have the butcher saw through the bones to make sirloin chops. You will end up with chops and a large leg of lamb for a roast or two, and still save a lot of money.

YOUR WAY You buy lamb steaks.

2 lbs. at $3.69 per lb. = $7.38

MY WAY I buy sirloin (large loin) lamb chops instead. These are also off the large loin and are just as tasty and tender as the steaks. They have more bone but are *much* less expensive.

2 lbs. at $3.29 per lb. = $6.58
SAVINGS $0.40 per lb.

TIP Ask your butcher for *hipper-dippers*. These are hip-bone lamb chops that come from between the small loin chops and the sirloin chops and are cheaper than either one. Hipper-dippers can be cut thin for chops, or thick (at least 1½ inches) for lamb blocks, which are small oven roasts. Besides, your butcher will wonder why it is that you know so much, and be a little bit more on his toes the next time you come in.

"Hipper-dipper" cut thick for an oven roast.

YOUR WAY You buy four rib chops—those delectable, small (expensive) chops.

¾ lb. at $3.79 per lb. = $2.85

MY WAY It's hard to save money buying rib chops, but I save a little by buying a whole rack of lamb, which is eight chops. I have the butcher cut it into chops, or do it myself (this is a simple job!). I freeze what I don't want—or invite a friend! These are not huge savings, but everything you can do helps when you get to the checkout stand.

1½ lbs. rack of lamb at $3.69 per lb. = $5.54
SAVINGS $0.10 per lb. and I have chops in the freezer.

TIP For best results cut the lamb chops at least one-inch thick.

"Make your own crown roast; save a fortune."

YOUR WAY   You buy a crown roast of lamb for a special, elegant dinner party. The butcher charges you a fortune to make it ($2.50 per chop!) since it takes up so much of his time.

Prepared crown roast = $60.00

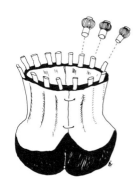

MY WAY   I make my own by buying three racks of lamb and asking the butcher to crack in between the bones so that at home I can bend each rack. I then ask the butcher to *french* the ends of the rib bones by removing the meat from the ends so that I can slip frills onto them. I already have on hand the frills, which I buy at a gourmet shop, six feet of string, a roll of aluminum foil, and a large bunch of parsley.

This is how to make your own crown roast:

1. Lay the three racks of lamb in a long row on the table.

2. About two inches from the bottom of the first rack, put a needle threaded with the string between the rib bones. Cross over to rack 2 and do the same. Pull the string tight to connect the racks. Now connect racks 2 and 3 the same way.

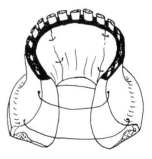

3. Repeat this operation at the top, pulling together the racks there, about two inches from the top. Now the racks are tied together top and bottom into a long row.
4. Tie rack 1 to the end of rack 3, keeping the fat side on the inside of the crown. The roast is ready for the oven.

After the roast is cooked, wrap a 3-inch-wide strip of aluminum foil around the base of the rack and secure the ends with toothpicks. Place the white or colored chop frills on the top of each rib bone, and put the bunch of parsley in the middle of the crown.

Three racks of lamb (1½ lbs. per rack) at $3.69 per lb. = $16.60

SAVINGS $43.38

TIP A crown roast can also be made with two racks of lamb. It will not have quite the roundness that you get with three racks, but it can be done.

already prepared $60.00	Two-rack crown roast = $40.00
3 racks cost 16.60	Two racks of lamb = $11.07
SAVINGS $43.40	**SAVINGS** = $28.92

YOUR WAY You buy lamb shoulder chops to broil for dinner.

2 lbs. at $2.39 per lb. = $4.78

MY WAY I ask the butcher for a whole five-rib shoulder roast. Then I have him cut it into blade and round-bone chops; the end piece can be cut for stew. You have to ask for this roast because you never see it in the counter. The butcher prefers to cut chops off the shoulder roast and sell them for a higher price per pound. But if you ask, you can get it. I save on the chops and get three good meals from this roast.

5 lbs. shoulder roast at $2.09 per lb. = $10.45

SAVINGS $0.30 per lb.

If you buy separately the same thing that I have cut from the 5-rib shoulder roast, here's what you pay:

2 lbs. shoulder lamb chops at $2.39 per lb. = $ 4.78

2 lbs. round-bone chops at $3.19 per lb. = $ 6.38

1 lb. lamb stew at $0.89 per lb. = $ 0.89

Total cost = $12.05

SAVINGS $ 1.60

TIP Lamb blocks, cut 1½ or 2 inches thick from the shoulder of the lamb, make lovely small oven roasts that are very economical. This is a cut from the old school and you don't often see it any more. But ask for lamb blocks, and if your butcher knows how to cut them they are delicious.

Lamb blocks

YOUR WAY You buy boneless chunks of lamb to make shish kabobs.

1 lb. lamb kabobs at $3.79 per lb. = $3.79

MY WAY I buy a 5-rib shoulder roast and ask the butcher to bone it. Then I cut it into cubes and remove the fat. Even if the butcher charges extra to bone the roast, it's still cheaper than buying boneless kabobs.

1 lb. kabobs cut from shoulder roast at $2.09 per lb. = $2.07

SAVINGS $1.70

TIP Try lamb riblets some day when you want an unusual taste treat. These are the small ends of the breast of lamb. They are quite cheap (usually under $1 per pound) and are wonderful baked in the oven or grilled over charcoal. There are not many riblets to a lamb, so it may be hard to find them. You can order them in advance (3-day notice, at least), or ask your butcher to freeze them and save them for you.

BARBECUED LAMB RIBLETS

3 lbs.	lamb riblets, trimmed of fat	¼ cup	molasses
1 tsp.	salt	1 cup	chili sauce
⅛ tsp.	pepper	2 tsp.	dried mustard
		1 clove	garlic, minced

Bring water to boil in large pot. Add riblets, salt and pepper. Cover and simmer for about 1 hour, or until tender. Meanwhile, in small saucepan, combine remaining ingredients and simmer over low heat for a few minutes. Remove lamb from water and brush with barbecue sauce. Grill 6-8 inches from hot coals, about 15 minutes on each side, brushing frequently with sauce. *Serves 4.*

MARINATED LAMB RIBLETS

3 lbs.	lamb riblets	¼ tsp.	rosemary
3 Tbsp.	olive oil	¼ tsp.	thyme
3 Tbsp.	soy sauce	½ tsp.	oregano
3 Tbsp.	water	1 Tbsp.	Worcestershire sauce
1 clove	garlic, minced		pepper

Marinate the riblets for 3 hours at room temperature. Barbecue or broil for 35-45 minutes, brushing occasionally with marinade.

YOUR WAY You buy boneless Saratoga lamb chops—an expensive, elegant cut. They are actually boneless small-loin lamb chops or boneless lamb steaks that have been wrapped in bacon.

3 lbs. Saratoga chops at $3.79 per lb. = $11.37

MY WAY I buy thick (1½-inch) sirloin lamb chops and cut out the bone myself. I then wrap bacon around the chops, secure it with toothpicks, and have the same elegant meal for almost half the price I would have paid to have the butcher do it. Again, you pay for labor, service, and convenience. Even throwing away the bone, or making soup stock out of it, I come out ahead.

3 lbs. sirloin chops at $3.29 per lb. = $9.87
SAVINGS $1.50 or $0.50 per lb.

Breast

TIP The lamb breast is one of the most economical cuts at the butcher's counter. It sells for $0.89 per pound (sometimes less). I think it is actually sweeter than the expensive leg of lamb at $2.49 per pound. It doesn't have as much eye appeal, however, and you do have to trim off some fat—perhaps that's why it's not more popular. Don't be deceived by its low price and its appearance; it is a versatile and tasty piece of meat.

BAKED LAMB BREAST

Season it with salt and pepper, rosemary, fresh garlic; squeeze on some lemon juice; and bake at 325 degrees for about one hour. Leave on some of the fat so it bastes itself; cut off excess fat after cooking.

You can also bone the breast by cutting along the ribs as close as you can come to the bone. Trim off fat. Roll up the meat like a jelly roll—with or without stuffing; tie strings around it and bake in the oven. Or you can cut it into 2-inch lamb rolls, secure with toothpicks, and broil. Wrap a slice of bacon around each lamb roll if you wish.

After boning the breast there is a small amount of meat left between the bones, which some people like to cook as spareribs.

YOUR WAY You buy chunks of lamb to make into stew. It is fatty and looks a bit dried out.

3 lbs. stew meat at $1.99 per lb. = $5.97

MY WAY I buy lamb neck, which is very cheap, and cut off the meat for the stew. (I could also use lamb shanks or lamb breast.) The chunks are lean, nice, and fresh, and cheaper even with the bone waste.

3 lbs. lamb neck at $0.99 per lb. = $2.67
SAVINGS $3.30 or $1.10 per lb.

Neck

Shank

Breast

YOUR WAY You buy a package of ground lamb to make patties or to add to a meat loaf. When you cook it you find that it is very fatty.

1 lb. ground lamb at $1.79 per lb. = $1.79

MY WAY I grind my own lamb for the same reason I grind most of my meats: I like to know what's in it. And I like it to be lean, so I use the lean meat from the lamb neck or breast or shank.

1 lb. lamb neck or breast at $0.89 per lb. = $0.89
SAVINGS $0.90 per lb.

Doing that extra work yourself saves you 50 percent and you really get what you want.

TIP Did you know that some markets add a little ground beef to the ground lamb? Ground lamb has a pale color, and ground beef makes the meat look leaner. This is not legal but is sometimes done. Another reason to grind your own.

REGGIE'S LAMB ROSETTES

1 lb.	ground lamb
1 clove	fresh garlic, minced
1	green onion, chopped
pinch	oregano
pinch	rosemary

salt and pepper
sliced bacon

Mix lamb and seasoning; shape into balls. Wrap a piece of bacon around each ball and secure with toothpicks. Broil or barbecue. Delicious!

Using "My Way" you can save on each lamb purchase—sometimes just a few pennies, but often a considerable amount of money—if you:

- Buy larger cuts (like the whole leg or shoulder roast) and ask the butcher to cut what you want,
- Try lesser-known cuts, like sirloin chops, lamb riblets, and lamb breast,
- Make your own crown roast,
- Cut your own stew meat and kabobs,
- Grind lamb at home.

Read on and save more dollars.

PORK

PORK is exceptionally high in nutritional value and is often a very good buy. Like lamb, pork is usually produced from young animals, so the quality varies less than with beef. There are only two grades for pork: *acceptable* and *unacceptable* (which is soft, watery meat).

You won't find the variety of fresh pork cuts that you find in beef because a good percentage of the meat is cured or processed and packaged in hams, bacon, canned meat, and so on. Most fresh cuts come from the pork loin.

When you buy pork, look for cuts with firm meat, little fat, and a small amount of marbling. The color should be grayish-pink. Pork that is red has been swill-fed and the flavor of the meat will not be so good.

Pork is generally cheaper during the summer months, although spareribs can be more expensive when demand is high during the barbecue season. Buy pork roasts during the summer and freeze them.

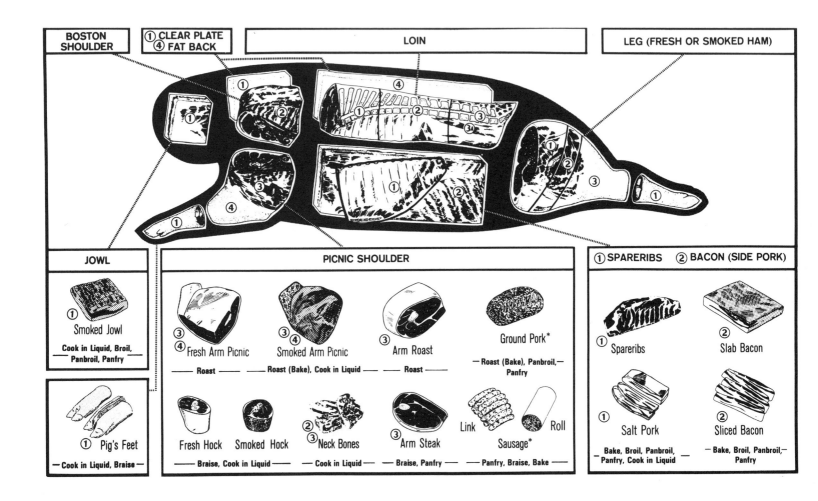

BOSTON SHOULDER

① CLEAR PLATE ④ FAT BACK

LOIN

LEG (FRESH OR SMOKED HAM)

JOWL

① Smoked Jowl

Cook in Liquid, Broil, Panbroil, Panfry

① Pig's Feet

— **Cook in Liquid, Braise** —

PICNIC SHOULDER

③
④ Fresh Arm Picnic

③
④ Smoked Arm Picnic

③ Arm Roast

Ground Pork*

— **Roast** —   — **Roast (Bake), Cook in Liquid** —   — **Roast** —

— **Roast (Bake), Panbroil,** —
Panfry

Fresh Hock

Smoked Hock

②
③ Neck Bones

③ Arm Steak

Link

Roll

Sausage*

— **Braise, Cook in Liquid** —   — **Cook in Liquid** —   — **Braise, Panfry** —   — **Panfry, Braise, Bake** —

① SPARERIBS   ② BACON (SIDE PORK)

① Spareribs

② Slab Bacon

① Salt Pork

② Sliced Bacon

— **Bake, Broil, Panbroil,** —
Panfry, Cook in Liquid

— **Bake, Broil, Panbroil,** —
Panfry

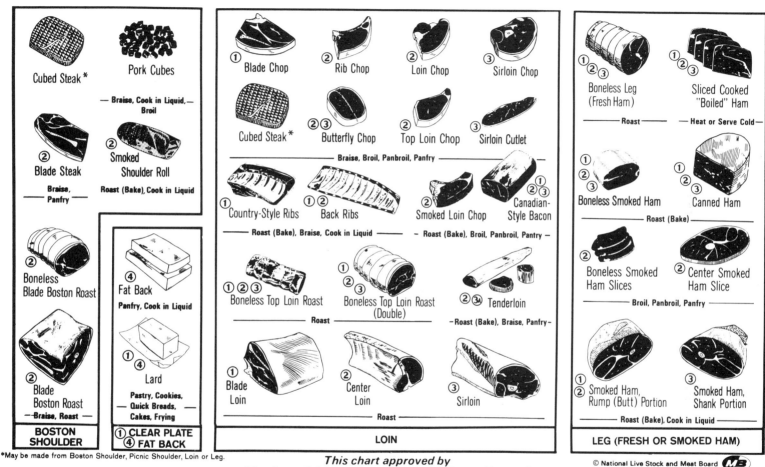

Cubed Steak *

Pork Cubes

— Braise, Cook in Liquid,—
Broil

② **Blade Steak**

Braise,
Panfry

② **Smoked Shoulder Roll**

Roast (Bake), Cook in Liquid

② **Boneless Blade Boston Roast**

② **Blade Boston Roast**

— Braise, Roast —

BOSTON SHOULDER

④ **Fat Back**

Panfry, Cook in Liquid

①④ **Lard**

Pastry, Cookies,
— Quick Breads,
Cakes, Frying

① **CLEAR PLATE**
④ **FAT BACK**

*May be made from Boston Shoulder, Picnic Shoulder, Loin or Leg.

① **Blade Chop**

② **Rib Chop**

② **Loin Chop**

③ **Sirloin Chop**

② **Cubed Steak** *

②③ **Butterfly Chop**

② **Top Loin Chop**

③ **Sirloin Cutlet**

— Braise, Broil, Panbroil, Panfry —

① **Country-Style Ribs**

①② **Back Ribs**

② **Smoked Loin Chop**

②③ **Canadian-Style Bacon**

— Roast (Bake), Braise, Cook in Liquid —

— Roast (Bake), Broil, Panbroil, Pantry —

①②③ **Boneless Top Loin Roast**

①② ③ **Boneless Top Loin Roast (Double)**

②③④ **Tenderloin**

— Roast —

— Roast (Bake), Braise, Panfry —

① **Blade Loin**

② **Center Loin**

③ **Sirloin**

— Roast —

LOIN

①②③ **Boneless Leg (Fresh Ham)**

①②③ **Sliced Cooked "Boiled" Ham**

— Roast —

— Heat or Serve Cold —

①②③ **Boneless Smoked Ham**

①②③ **Canned Ham**

— Roast (Bake) —

② **Boneless Smoked Ham Slices**

② **Center Smoked Ham Slice**

— Broil, Panbroil, Panfry —

①② **Smoked Ham, Rump (Butt) Portion**

③ **Smoked Ham, Shank Portion**

— Roast (Bake), Cook in Liquid —

LEG (FRESH OR SMOKED HAM)

This chart approved by
National Live Stock and Meat Board

© National Live Stock and Meat Board **M3**

Pork chart / 93

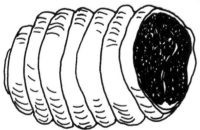

YOUR WAY   You buy a boneless loin of pork roast.

5 lbs. at $2.99 per lb. = $14.95

MY WAY   I buy two blade-end pork roasts at about 3 pounds each. I ask the butcher to lift off the shoulder blade bones and throw them away, then bone out the ribs and throw away the ''rough'' portion (the back bones), saving the ribs for me. There will be about 1 pound of waste. I also ask the butcher for a piece of *jet net*—they are usually happy to give this to you—or some string.

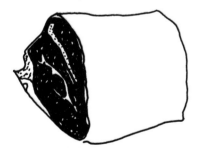

If the butcher does not provide this service free, try to bone the roast yourself. It's not difficult to do (see illustration) and is a real money-saver. (Don't try to do this with a loin-end roast—it's very difficult to bone out!)

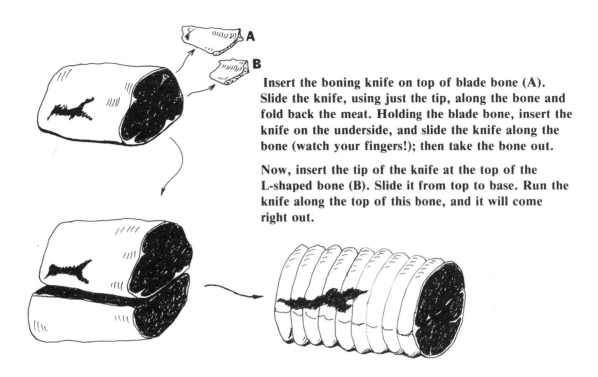

Insert the boning knife on top of blade bone (A). Slide the knife, using just the tip, along the bone and fold back the meat. Holding the blade bone, insert the knife on the underside, and slide the knife along the bone (watch your fingers!); then take the bone out.

Now, insert the tip of the knife at the top of the L-shaped bone (B). Slide it from top to base. Run the knife along the top of this bone, and it will come right out.

When I get home I lay out the two roasts. Each one tapers, with one end smaller than the other. I lay one roast on top of the other, with the small end on top of the large end so the roast will have good, even conformation. I slip the net over the roasts or tie string around them, and I've got my boneless pork loin roast.

The leftover rib bones have meat between them. I use them as pork riblets, or I bone them out and use the meat in a Chinese dish.

Two 3-lb. blade-end pork roasts at $1.59 per lb. = $9.54

SAVINGS $5.41

For a smaller boneless roast, you can buy just one blade-end roast and have it boned and tied.

YOUR WAY You buy a pork tenderloin (the "cream" of the pork loin) which is an expensive piece of meat.

1½ lbs. at $3.29 per lb. = $4.94

MY WAY I beat the high price of pork tenderloin by making my own. I buy the sirloin half of the pork loin (about 8 pounds) and take out the tenderloin. It's not difficult if you follow my illustration. I use the rest of the sirloin as a roast, cut it into chops, or dice and use it in other dishes.

The tenderloin lies next to the bone and resembles a small eye roast. Insert the tip of the boning knife at the large end of the roast, between the bone and the tenderloin. Slide the knife along the bone, and the fillet will separate easily from the rest of the roast.

1½ lbs. loin of pork roast at $1.59 per lb. = $2.39

SAVINGS $2.55

For a smaller tenderloin roast (enough for two people), buy a loin-end roast and remove the tenderloin. You will end up with about ¾ pound.

TIP Blade-end roast and loin-end roast are usually the same price. The loin end is the better buy because it contains the fillet (the tenderloin).

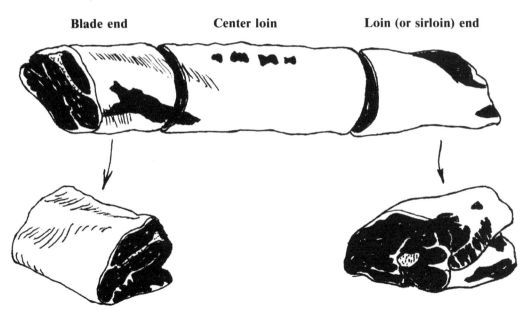

Blade end   **Center loin**   **Loin (or sirloin) end**

"Slice your own pork chops."

YOUR WAY You buy center-cut pork chops, thin-sliced, about ¼-inch thick.

3 lbs. center-cut chops at $2.49 per lb. = $7.47

Loin end

MY WAY I buy an end-cut loin of pork roast and ask the butcher to crack the bones about ¼-inch thick. At home I slice the roast into chops—and save almost half by doing the slicing myself! Chops from the end-cut loin are not quite so lean as center-cut chops and have more bone, but they are every bit as tasty—and much cheaper.

3 lbs. end-cut loin roast at $1.59 per lb. = $4.77

SAVINGS $0.90 per lb.
$2.70 for 3 lbs.

Blade end

TIP Don't be fooled into thinking you're getting a bargain in "family packs" or a package of "assorted chops." You save more money by buying an end-cut loin roast, or a whole or half loin of pork.

YOUR WAY   You buy smoked pork chops and you pay more because of the smoking process.

MY WAY   I buy a loin of pork and cut it into chops (see previous page), then "smoke" the chops myself. I rub the chops with bottled liquid smoke, put them in a plastic bag, and place them in the refrigerator for a few hours or overnight. The chops acquire a nice smoked flavor. You can also get the same smoky taste by adding some of the liquid smoke to the pan oil when you fry your chops, or by adding liquid smoke to your marinade or barbecue sauce.

Smoked pork chops are about $0.20 per pound more, so that is my saving.

The chapter on smoking meats tells more about liquid smoke preparations and how to prepare meats with them. See page 175.

YOUR WAY You buy meaty country-style ribs to barbecue.

3 lbs. country-style ribs at $1.69 per lb. = $5.07

MY WAY I buy a 3- to 4-pound blade-end loin pork roast—these are often on sale—and ask the butcher to cut it into country-style ribs. Or, I do it myself. It's an easy job since the roast is already cut through the bone (see illustration).

3 lbs. blade-end roast at $1.59 per lb. = $4.77
SAVINGS $0.30

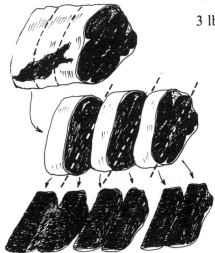

"You can save a bundle by buying a whole loin of pork."

YOUR WAY   When the whole loin of pork (about 16 pounds) is cut up by the butcher and put on the counter, this is what he cuts and what you buy:

$$
\begin{array}{rcl}
\text{3 lbs. loin-end roast at \$1.59 per lb.} &=& \$ \ 4.77 \\
\text{4 lbs. center-cut chops at \$2.29 per lb.} &=& \$ \ 9.16 \\
\text{3 lbs. thin center-cut chops at \$2.49 per lb.} &=& \$ \ 7.47 \\
\text{3 lbs. boneless rib chops at \$3.29 per lb.} &=& \$ \ 9.87 \\
\text{3 lbs. country-style spareribs at \$1.69 per lb.} &=& \$ \ 5.07 \\
& & \text{Total} \quad \$36.34
\end{array}
$$

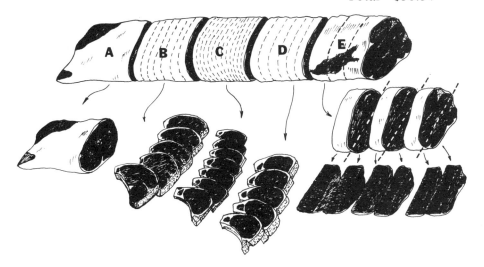

A   Loin-end roast
B   Center-cut chops
C   Thin chops
D   Boneless chops
E   Country-style spareribs

MY WAY I buy a whole loin of pork and ask the butcher to cut it for me. (Be sure to check with the butcher beforehand. Most will do this as a free service, but make sure.)

I ask the butcher to cut the following:

1. One 3-pound loin pork roast, cracking the bones to make the roast easier to carve.
2. Cut about 3 pounds of the ribs into one piece. When I get home, I remove the bones by just running a knife along the rib bones. Then I slice into boneless chops.
3. Cut about 7 pounds of center-cut pork chops, 3 pounds thinly sliced, and 4 pounds regular.
4. Cut about 3 pounds of country-style spareribs.

16 lbs. whole pork loin at $1.55 per lb. = $24.80

SAVINGS $11.54

Your Way	$36.34
My Way	24.80
SAVINGS	$11.54

TIP If you can't afford to buy the whole pork loin, you can buy half a loin (loin end, not blade) for the same price per pound. Ask the butcher to cut it into chops.

"Whole pork shoulders are a good value—lots of sweet and flavorful meat."

YOUR WAY   You buy pork butt steaks, already sliced and packaged.

4 lbs. pork butt steaks at $1.98 per lb. = $ 7.92

MY WAY   I buy a pork butt roast (also called a Boston shoulder), whole or half, and have the butcher cut it into steaks. They are very sweet and just as tender as loin pork chops. The butt half has more meat, less bone, and is more expensive than the shoulder half, but the butt is always available. A fresh shoulder half has to be ordered.

4 lbs. pork butt roast at $1.69 per lb. = $6.76
SAVINGS $1.16

**Butt roast
(Boston shoulder)**

YOUR WAY   You buy diced pork to make a Chinese dish.

2 lbs. pork cubes at $1.98 per lb. = $3.96

MY WAY   I dice my own pork, using slices of pork butt steak or steaks that I cut from a pork butt roast. I also check the price of loin-end roasts. If they are cheaper, then that's what I use.

2 lbs. pork steak at $1.69 per lb. = $3.38
SAVINGS $0.58

**Butt roast
(Boston shoulder)**

**Shoulder roast
(fresh picnic)**

TIP You can save even more by buying a whole pork shoulder or butt, if you can get the butcher to bone it for you (some do, some won't). If the butcher won't bone it for you, I don't recommend tackling a pork shoulder at home. It's difficult—and dangerous unless you've very good with a knife and have the right knife. You might try boning a pork butt—the bone is small, so the job is easier. The boneless meat can then be used for stew, Chinese dishes, kabobs, or ground coarsely and used for pork sausage.

Try using pork for shish kabobs instead of the more expensive beef or lamb.

CURRIED PORK KABOBS

(Laurent Welter, Frenchy's Gourmet Meats, Novato, California)

Combine in a bowl:

1 cup	lemon juice	½ tsp.	salt
2 Tbsp.	curry powder	2	small onions, grated
1 Tbsp.	soy sauce	few dashes Tabasco	
1 tsp.	sugar		

Marinate 2 pounds of lean pork cubes in the mixture for several hours. Place on skewers with chunks of green pepper. Broil, turning frequently, until pork is thoroughly cooked. Serve with rice and curry condiments such as chopped scallions, and chutney.

YOUR WAY   You buy pork cube steaks to fry for a quick dinner.

2 lbs. cube steaks at $2.39 per lb. = $4.78

MY WAY   I make cube steaks out of pork butt steaks. I take out the bone, then mold the meat together by pounding it between two pieces of waxed paper. Then I score both sides horizontally and vertically.

2 lbs. pork butt at $1.69 per lb. = $3.38
SAVINGS $1.40

HERB-SEASONED PORK STEAKS

4 pork cube steaks	1 cup herb-seasoned stuffing
2-4 Tbsp. shortening	mix, crushed
1 egg	¼ cup grated Parmesan
3 Tbsp. milk	cheese

In pie plate, beat egg and milk with a fork until combined. In another pie plate, combine stuffing mix and cheese; mix well. Dip steaks in egg mixture, then in crumb mixture. Cook in hot shortening over medium heat for 5 to 7 minutes. Turn and cook the other side until browned. *4 servings.*

Butt roast

YOUR WAY   You buy the butt portion of a fresh pork leg, which makes a delicious roast.

4 lbs. at $1.49 per lb. = $5.96

MY WAY   I buy a whole pork leg (about 13 pounds). It costs less per pound, and I also get the three center-cut leg steaks that are always removed because they sell for so much more.

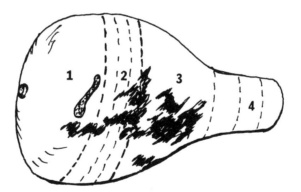

I ask the butcher to do the following for me:

1. Remove the butt roast.

Butt roast

2. Cut the three steaks off the leg.

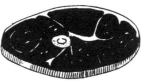

Steaks

3. Cut a shank-leg roast.

Shank-leg roast

4. Cut three shank pieces (hocks), which I use to flavor beans.

Shank pieces (hock)

You can save a lot of money by buying the whole leg, having it cut as I outline above, then freezing what you don't want right away. When you buy everything separately, you pay this:

4 lbs. butt portion roast at $1.49 per lb.	= $ 5.96
Three 1-lb. steaks at $2.09 per lb.	= $ 6.27
5 lbs. shank-leg roast at $1.39 per lb.	= $ 6.85
1 lb. hocks at $1.19 per lb.	= $ 1.19
Total	= $20.27

But when you buy the whole leg and have it cut, you pay only:

Whole leg, 13 lbs. at $1.29 per lb.	= $16.77
SAVINGS	$ 3.50

If you don't want this much meat, you can buy half a leg for the same price per pound.

TIP You don't often see fresh pork leg on the counter. Most of them are used to make ham. But the butcher can always get one for you if you give him at least a 3-day notice.

"Pork is often on sale, so compare prices."

YOUR WAY You buy some ground pork. It is fatty, and when you cook it you lose almost half in grease.

MY WAY I make my own ground pork. I buy the blade end or sirloin end of pork loin, or a pork butt or shoulder, whichever is on sale for the cheapest price. I ask the butcher to bone it and grind it for me—or better yet, I grind it myself at home. Considering the loss in grease in packaged ground pork (about 50 percent), I can grind my own for about the same price or less, and the meat I get is much tastier and more nutritious.

TIP The bulk sausage sold today is not at all satisfactory. Even "name-brand" sausage can be quite fatty and usually contains chemicals and preservatives—read the label before you buy. Try grinding some pork and making your own sausage.

PORK SAUSAGE

2½ lbs. pork butt, boned and cubed	1 bunch green onions, chopped
½ lb. pork fat	1 bunch watercress, chopped (optional)
1 Tbsp. salt	1 tsp. each: dill, marjoram, rosemary, tarragon, thyme, oregano
pepper (to taste)	
1 Tbsp. caraway seeds	
1 Tbsp. sage	fresh garlic (to taste)
1 Tbsp. chopped parsley	

Grind meat and fat together; add herbs and spices and mix well. Chill overnight or freeze.

YOUR WAY You buy spareribs to barbecue or cook with sauerkraut.

3 lbs. spareribs at $1.49 per lb. = $4.47

MY WAY I buy pork neck bones. The bones are shaped differently, but they cook and taste like spareribs, and sell for half the price. I order them in advance from the butcher because he doesn't usually carry them.

3 lbs. neck bones at $0.68 per lb. = $2.04
SAVINGS $2.43

It cost me less than half.

TIP Pigs' feet are a great economy meal. There's a lot of waste, but the price per pound is ridiculously low. Pigs' feet must usually be ordered in advance. Be sure to ask the butcher to crack them on the saw when you buy them. See page 190 for a really special dish—tripe with pigs' feet.

Pork is a good value, and now you know how to make it a better value by:

- Watching for those super sales;
- Making your own boneless roasts;
- Slicing your own chops and country-style ribs;
- Buying a whole loin or a whole leg, asking the butcher to cut it the way you want it, and filling your freezer;
- Making your own diced pork, cube steaks, and ground pork;
- Trying new economy cuts, like pork neck bones and pigs' feet.

Pork may not always be as inexpensive as it is today, but you'll still save money if you buy My Way.

VEAL

THERE is not much to say about saving money on veal—it is the most expensive meat in the market! Veal is good for you, however, since it has little or no fat, is high in nutritional value, and is low in cholesterol. And there *are* some ways to save money when you buy it.

Always watch for sales and load up your freezer when the prices are low. The rule of buying larger cuts versus small cuts will save you money, and in this chapter I will tell you about a few economical cuts. You may have trouble getting certain cuts because many markets carry only a limited selection. Veal is so expensive that it is not a fast seller. However, most butchers will order special cuts for you if you give advance notice.

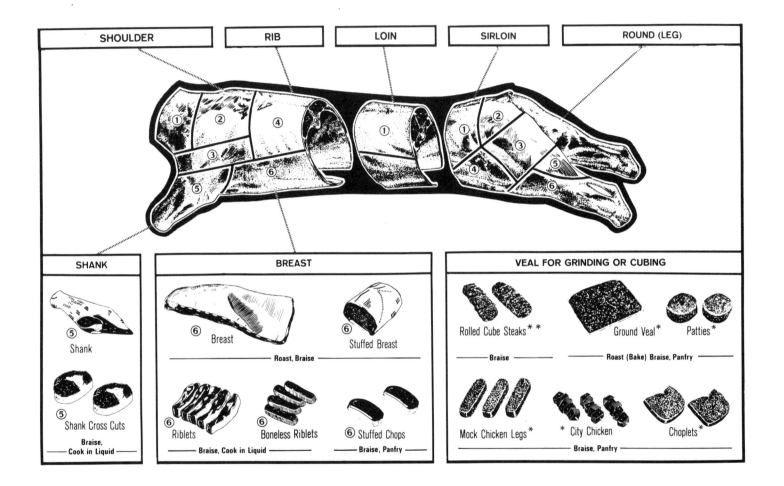

| SHOULDER | RIB | LOIN | SIRLOIN | ROUND (LEG) |

SHANK

⑤ Shank

⑤ Shank Cross Cuts

Braise,
Cook in Liquid

BREAST

⑥ Breast

⑥ Stuffed Breast

Roast, Braise

⑥ Riblets

⑥ Boneless Riblets

⑥ Stuffed Chops

Braise, Cook in Liquid   **Braise, Panfry**

VEAL FOR GRINDING OR CUBING

Rolled Cube Steaks **

Ground Veal*   Patties*

Braise   **Roast (Bake) Braise, Panfry**

Mock Chicken Legs *

* City Chicken

Choplets *

Braise, Panfry

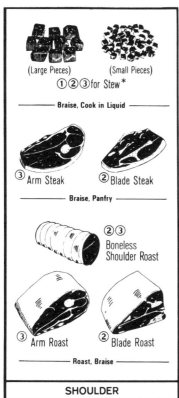

(Large Pieces)   (Small Pieces)

①②③ for Stew*

— Braise, Cook in Liquid —

③ Arm Steak   ② Blade Steak

— Braise, Panfry —

②③ Boneless Shoulder Roast

③ Arm Roast   ② Blade Roast

— Roast, Braise —

SHOULDER

④ Boneless Rib Chop

④ Rib Chop

— Braise, Panfry —

④ Crown Roast

④ Rib Roast

— Roast —

RIB

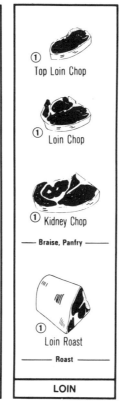

① Top Loin Chop

① Loin Chop

① Kidney Chop

— Braise, Panfry —

① Loin Roast

— Roast —

LOIN

Cubed Steak**

① Sirloin Chop

— Braise, Panfry —

Boneless Sirloin Roast

① Sirloin Roast

— Roast —

SIRLOIN

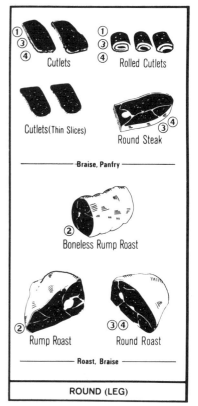

① ③ ④ Cutlets   ① ③ ④ Rolled Cutlets

Cutlets (Thin Slices)   ③ ④ Round Steak

— Braise, Panfry —

② Boneless Rump Roast

② Rump Roast   ③ ④ Round Roast

— Roast, Braise —

ROUND (LEG)

*Veal for stew or grinding may be made from any cut.

**Cube steaks may be made from any thick solid piece of boneless veal.

This chart approved by
National Live Stock and Meat Board

Veal chart / 115

YOUR WAY   You buy veal cutlets (thin steaks from the leg) to saute or to make veal parmesan.

1 lb. veal cutlets at $5.69 per lb. = $5.69

MY WAY   I buy a leg of veal (about 4 pounds) and have the butcher cut it into cutlets. Or I ask the butcher to bone it out (the bone weighs about a pound), and then I cut it into steaks myself. (Put it in the freezer for about an hour to firm it up so it's easier to cut.)

4 lb. leg of veal at $3.79 = $15.16
(and I could get it on sale for less)

I get 3 pounds of veal cutlets for $15.16;
you'd pay $17.07 for 3 pounds.

SAVINGS $1.91

TIP   You can cut part of a leg of veal into cutlets and tie the rest together for a rolled roast.

YOUR WAY You buy thinly sliced veal to make scallopini, and you pay a high price.

> 1 lb. scallopini at $5.69 per lb. = $5.69

MY WAY I take the steaks that I cut from the leg of veal and use a meat slicer or sharp knife to cut them very thin. Then I put the meat between sheets of waxed paper and pound it thinner.

> 1 lb. scallopini sliced from leg steaks at $3.79 per lb. = $3.79
> **SAVINGS** $1.90 per lb.

YOUR WAY You buy veal steaks cut from the leg. They are very expensive.

> 2 lbs. veal steaks at $5.69 per lb. = $11.38

MY WAY I buy sirloin (large loin) veal chops, choosing the ones with the smallest bones. I either have the butcher remove the bone or I remove it myself. If I want the chops thinner, I pound them between waxed paper. Sirloin chops taste just as good as veal steak. The bone is bigger, but the difference in price more than makes up for it.

> 2 lbs. sirloin chops at $3.19 per lb. = $6.38
> **SAVINGS** $5.00
> (or $2.50 per lb.)

TIP To save on a crown roast of veal, make it yourself. Follow the directions for crown roast of lamb, page 81.

YOUR WAY You want a veal roast, so you buy a boneless sirloin tip. Even on sale this roast is expensive.

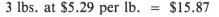

3 lbs. at $5.29 per lb. = $15.87

MY WAY I buy a boneless shoulder roast. I ask the butcher to wrap it in pork fat so it bastes itself as it roasts and does not get dry. You can baste it a little extra with white wine for added flavor. It's a delicious, inexpensive roast, and there's no waste.

Boneless shoulder roast

3 lbs. shoulder roast at $2.19 per lb. = $6.57

SAVINGS $9.30

Or you can do it a little differently and save even more:

MY WAY Breast of veal also makes a lovely roast. I buy a breast and ask the butcher to cut a pocket in it. Then I stuff it with a ground-veal, spinach or chard, and bread-crumb stuffing. (You can also bake it unstuffed.)

Breast

$$
\begin{array}{rl}
\text{3 lbs. breast of veal at \$1.29 per lb.} & = \quad \$3.87 \\
\text{1 lb. ground veal for stuffing at \$1.79 per lb.} & = \quad \$1.79 \\
\hline
& \quad \$\ 5.66 \\
\textbf{SAVINGS} & \quad \$10.21
\end{array}
$$

The breast will have about 1 pound of bone, but my savings are so enormous that I'm still ahead of the game.

TIP The breast is the most economical cut of veal. You can bake it, cook it on the grill (basting with wine, garlic and seasonings), or cut it between the ribs to make riblets. You can also use the meat for stew.

STUFFED BREAST OF VEAL

3 lbs.	breast of veal	¼ cup	fresh parsley, chopped
1 lb.	ground veal	1 tsp.	thyme
1 cup	fresh chard or spinach, chopped	1 tsp.	oregano
1 cup	bread cubes	2	eggs
½ cup	finely chopped onion	1 tsp.	salt
1	fresh garlic clove, finely chopped	¼ tsp.	pepper

Ask the butcher to cut a pocket in the breast of veal. Mix the other ingredients. Stuff the pocket of veal and sew it securely. Brush with melted butter. Roast for about 2½ hours or to an internal temperature of 160 degrees. *Delicious!*

YOUR WAY You buy veal cube steaks, tenderized and ready to cook.

2 lbs. at $3.99 per lb. = $7.98

MY WAY I buy round-bone shoulder veal chops. There is some bone waste, so I buy a little more than 2 pounds. I bone it, remove the fat and skin, score the meat on both sides horizontally and vertically, and they are ready to go.

2¼ lbs. shoulder chops at $2.19 per lb. = $4.93

SAVINGS $3.05

TIP Try shoulder veal chops instead of rib chops. They taste as good and are about 20 cents a pound cheaper.

Rib chops   **Shoulder chops**

YOUR WAY You buy a package of ground veal to use for stuffing a breast or to add to a meat loaf.

> 1 lb. ground veal at $1.79 per lb. = $1.79

MY WAY I buy a veal breast and bone it out and grind it myself. (Boning is simple, just run your knife along the bone.) The bones in a veal breast are small and light, so you don't lose much in weight.

> 1 lb. veal breast at $1.29 per lb. = $1.29
> **SAVINGS** $0.50 per lb.

YOUR WAY You buy a package of veal stew meat. You don't really know what cut of veal it comes from.

1 lb. stew meat at $2.19 per lb. = $2.19

MY WAY I buy a veal boneless shoulder roast or breast, whichever is cheaper, and cut the stew meat myself. It's less expensive and better!

1 lb. shoulder roast at $2.19 per lb. = $2.19
or 1 lb. breast at $1.29 per lb. = $1.29
SAVINGS up to $0.90 per lb.

TIP Calf's feet are wonderful for enriching soup stock because they provide gelatin. Usually they must be ordered in advance. Ask the butcher to crack them on the saw.

Veal doesn't have to be out of sight when you buy "My Way":

- Have the butcher cut cutlets and scallopini from a leg of veal.
- Substitute less expensive cuts: large loin chops instead of steaks, shoulder chops for rib chops, shoulder roast for sirloin tip.
- Try breast of veal—the most economical cut.
- Make your own cube steak, stew meat, and ground veal.

I hope that by now you're buying meat much differently—and saving lots of money.

POULTRY

DOLLAR per pound, poultry is an excellent value compared with other meats—and there are ways you can save even more money on it. If you're really interested in saving money, try cutting up your poultry yourself—it's *not* difficult. Some shops cut up chicken or turkey for you at no extra charge, but most do not because it is such a time-consuming job. Again, it's important to check your store's policy.

Also, know your terms when you buy poultry. For example, *broilers* are chickens that weigh 2½ pounds or less, *frying chickens* or *fryers* are about 3 to 4½ pounds, and *roasters* are 5 to 6 pounds. *Stewers, fricassee,* or *hens* refer to older chickens that must be cooked long and slowly. Don't be taken in by made-up names: an "old-fashioned hen" is nothing more than a stewing chicken—tough and old. And beware of shops that take a large frying chicken, label it a "roaster," and charge you 10 cents a pound more. A roaster should weigh at least 5 pounds; don't pay more for simply a large fryer.

WING TAGS

Look for the *grade identification label* and for the *inspection seal.* The grades for dressed and ready-to-cook poultry are A, B, and C.

Grade A poultry has perfect conformation—rounded and well covered with flesh; is free of deformities; free of pin feathers; with no cuts, tears, or broken bones, and no discoloration or darkening or drying due to freezing.

Grade B may have some deformities (crooked breast or back or misshapen legs or wings); has a moderate covering of flesh and fat; may have a few pinfeathers; may have some cuts and tears; may have disjointed parts or parts of wing or tail removed; may have slight discolorations or freezing defects.

Grade C does not meet the requirements for grade B; for example, wings may be removed, breast and legs may be trimmed, and so on.

When you buy poultry, remember that you are buying a frame of bones. The larger bird is a better buy because the yield will be higher; that is, there will be more meat in proportion to bones.

One of the best ways to save money is to buy whole chickens and cut them up yourself. It takes practice, but is not difficult to learn. Use a sharp boning knife, or poultry shears, and follow these simple directions. Don't be chicken!

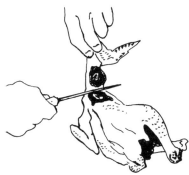

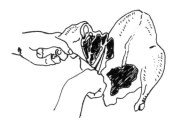

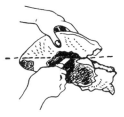

1   Cut off wings by cutting around the base, then through the joint. (To find the joint, move the wing up and down.) If desired, cut wing into two pieces, cutting through the joint.

2   Next, remove the leg and thigh. Cut around the thigh, close to the body; bend the leg back to expose the joint. Insert blade and cut down. To separate the leg from the thigh, wiggle it to find the joint, then cut through it.

3   To remove the breast, insert knife in body cavity and cut along the bottom edge of the ribs. Repeat on the other side, then break away the breast section from the back. Cut the breast in half, if desired.

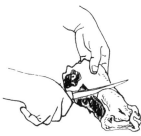

4   Cut the back in half at the end of the rib cage.

To quarter a chicken, don't worry about finding the joints. Insert the knife about one inch and cut along the spinal column. Then cut the chicken into quarters, as shown in the following illustrations:

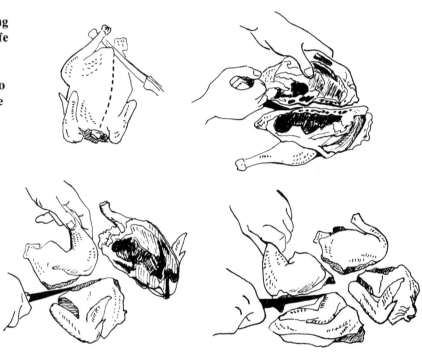

YOUR WAY   You buy some chicken legs and breasts to fry for a picnic.

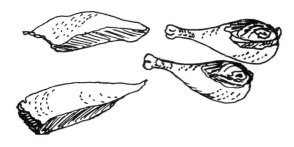

½ lb. legs at $1.39 per lb. = $0.70
1 lb. breasts at $1.49 per lb. = $1.49
Total $2.19

MY WAY   When I take home chicken, it's never parts—it's the whole chicken. Then I cut it up myself. I fry the legs and breasts and save the other parts for another dinner.

Legs and breasts $2.19
3 lbs. whole chicken at $0.79 per lb. = $2.37

SAVINGS   I paid about the same and got what you did, *plus* 2 thighs, 2 wings, and other parts for soup or the next dinner.

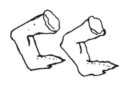

TIP Even if your family likes only the legs and breasts, there are ways to use the other parts:

- Make soup or stew out of the wings, backs and necks (there's plenty of meat on them). Or you can boil them, pull off the meat, and make chicken salad.

- Grind the gizzards and hearts and use the meat to stretch your spaghetti sauce. Just add to the ground beef.

- Freeze the wings, and when you have a bunch, fry them up for hors d'oeuvres or for snacks for hungry kids.

POOR MAN'S SPAGHETTI SAUCE

Use your favorite recipe for spaghetti sauce, but substitute ground chicken gizzards and hearts for one half of the meat. You won't notice a difference in taste and it will be a real money saver.

TIP If you absolutely cannot cut up a chicken, cook the chicken whole. It will then pull or cut apart easily and you can serve the parts.

CHICKEN AND RICE

(I'll take credit for this recipe myself. I made it up and have enjoyed it many times.)

1	whole frying chicken or 10 chicken wings	2 cups	rice
½	bell pepper, chopped	1 can	chicken broth
2	fresh lemons		parsley, chopped
1 cube	butter		salt and pepper to taste

Melt butter and combine with lemon juice. Pour on chicken and bake at 325 degrees for about an hour. Add bell peppers for the last ten minutes. Cook rice with chicken broth in separate pot. Add parsley to rice when it's almost done. Pull chicken meat from the bones and dice up. Place rice, chicken, and pan drippings in a frying pan. Cover and warm for about ten minutes.

YOUR WAY You love boneless chicken breasts and use them in many different recipes.

¾ lb. at $2.98 per lb. = $2.25

MY WAY I buy a whole-body chicken, cut it up, and bone the breasts myself. I freeze the rest of the chicken to use later for a fried chicken dinner and for soup.

3 lbs. whole chicken at $0.79 per lb. = $2.37

SAVING You paid for a whole chicken and only got two breasts!

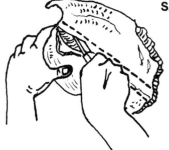

To bone a chicken breast, cut along each side of the breastbone.

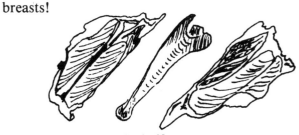

Using the knife, or your fingers, loosen the meat and pull it off the breastbone.

TIP If you are not sure of yourself the first time you bone the breast, cook the chicken first. After it is cooked, gently pull the bone from the breast, and the boneless meat is ready to slice and use in an elegant recipe.

Compare prices between whole and cut-up chickens, and you will see that it does not pay to buy chicken parts:

Breasts	1 lb. at $1.49	= $1.49
Thighs	½ lb. at $1.39	= $0.70
Legs	½ lb. at $1.39	= $0.70
Wings	¼ lb. at $0.89	= $0.23
Backs and necks	½ lb. at $0.39	= $0.20
Liver, hearts, and gizzards (Butchers call this the "motor")	¼ lb. at $1.19	= $0.30
	Total	= $3.62

versus

Whole chicken	3 lbs. at $0.79	= $2.37

And compare the price of buying chickens already cut up:

Split chickens
Cut-up chickens $0.98 per lb.

versus

Whole chickens $0.79 per lb.
You'll save up to $0.20 per lb.

When you buy whole chickens and see how much money you save, you'll never switch back.

YOUR WAY You want to make chicken soup, so you buy a stewing chicken.

3 lbs. at $0.85 per lb. = $2.55

MY WAY I buy chicken necks and backs, or use some that I've saved in the freezer. They are very cheap, have quite a lot of meat on them, and make a delicious soup.

3 lbs. necks and backs at $0.39 per lb. = $1.17
SAVINGS $1.38

TIP Don't buy a stewing chicken without checking the price of fryers first. Sometimes you can buy a fryer for less than a stewing chicken. It will make just as good a soup—just don't cook it so long (and besides, this will save on energy!).

Turkey

YOUR WAY You buy a 12-pound turkey. Your family of four gets four meals out of it.

12 lbs. at $0.98 per lb. = $11.76

MY WAY I always pick the largest turkey because the yield will be best. So I buy a 20-pound turkey. I only pay $3.24 more than you do, $15.00, but my family gets ten meals out of it, plus a larger carcass to use for soup.

If I don't want to cook 20 pounds of turkey at one time, I ask the butcher to saw it in half lengthwise. I freeze one half and cook the other half.

Small turkey, $0.98 per lb., cost per meal = $2.94
Large turkey, $0.75 per lb., cost per meal = $1.50
SAVINGS $1.44 per meal

and I get six more meals!

TIP If you've never roasted a half-bodied turkey, here's what to do: skewer skin to meat along cut edges to prevent shrinkage; tie leg to tail and wing to breast with string. Brush skin with melted butter. Roast at 325 degrees 2½ to 3 hours for 5–8 pounds; 3 to 3½ hours for 8–10 pounds; 3½ to 4 hours for 10–12 pounds: this is about 20 minutes per pound. If you use a meat thermometer, insert it in the inside thigh muscle (be sure it's not touching the bone), roast until thermometer registers 180–185 degrees.

TIP If a hen turkey and a tom turkey are the same price, which one is the best buy? The tom is because there is more yield—more meat for your money. The best restaurants and hotels never buy hen turkeys because there isn't enough meat on them. They buy the largest tom turkeys (30–35 pounds). The meat is just as tender and tasty as with a hen.

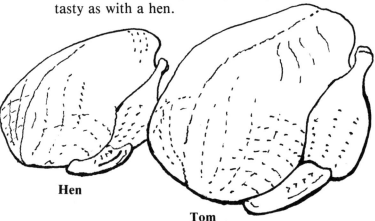

Hen

Tom

YOUR WAY You buy a self-basting turkey, thinking that it is sure to be juicier and tastier.

>   20-lb. self-basting turkey at $0.98 per lb. = $19.60

MY WAY I buy a large (20-pound) Grade A frozen turkey. When I roast it, I baste it myself with pure butter. It's just as tender and juicy as your turkey—in fact, mine is tastier because it is basted with butter, not vegetable oil. I read the label of one self-basting turkey to see what I would be paying $0.25 extra per pound for: vegetable oil, soybean and coconut oils, water, salt, emulsifiers, glycerides, polysorbate, artificial color, artificial flavor, 3 percent creamery butter (about a teaspoon!), sodium phosphates, lecithin, and sugar. You surely don't need all those oils and chemicals!

>   20-lb. turkey at $0.75 per lb. = $15.00
>   **SAVINGS** $4.60

Even adding in $0.90 or so for half a pound of butter, you come out way ahead.

For an extra juicy and tasty turkey (or chicken): Take a cube butter, melted, and the juice of two lemons (or white wine). Baste the turkey while it's cooking. Use an internal baster the last 15 minutes of cooking and inject mixture into each leg, wing, thigh, breast, and the back.

TIP A stuffed turkey is another poor buy. You pay about $0.50 per pound (or about $5.00 per 10 pounds) because the bird is stuffed. You can make stuffing for a lot less than that, and what's more, you can put in any ingredients you want!

YOUR WAY You order a fresh turkey far in advance so you'll have one for Thanksgiving. It costs you more, but you want to be sure it will be fresh and good.

20 lbs. at $0.95 per lb. = $19.00

MY WAY I buy a frozen turkey, thaw it properly (under refrigeration for about 24 hours) for Thanksgiving. It is tender, juicy, delicious, just as good as your fresh turkey—and I pay less.

20 lbs. at $0.75 per lb. = $15.00
SAVINGS $ 4.00

Remember, fresh turkeys are delivered many days before Thanksgiving. They go through many changes in temperature—from the plant, to the warehouse, to the truck, to the market, to the shopping cart, to the car, to the refrigerator, to the counter for stuffing. With each temperature change, the turkey bleeds, letting out a little more juice. This tends to make the turkey dry. A frozen turkey is frozen immediately after it is killed, and stays frozen until you bring it home and thaw it in the refrigerator.

Also, you often have to special order a fresh turkey. (For every fresh turkey that is sold, 75 to 100 frozen turkeys are sold.)

I'm not saying that a fresh turkey isn't good, but can you really tell the difference between fresh and frozen?

Compare the price of turkeys, and you'll see for yourself what the best buy is. (These are prices for 1980, but the best deal will be the best deal even when prices go up.)

Frozen tom turkey	$0.75 per lb. = $15.00	for a 20-lb. bird
Frozen hen turkey	$0.98 per lb. = $19.60	''
Fresh tom turkey	$0.95 per lb. = $19.00	''
Fresh hen turkey	$0.98 per lb. = $19.60	''
Self-basting turkey	$0.98 per lb. = $19.60	''
Junior turkey	$0.98 per lb. = $19.60	''
Stuffed turkey	$1.19 per lb. = $23.80	''
Smoked turkey	$1.29 per lb. = $25.80	''

TIP Don't buy frozen turkey rolls. They're a guaranteed disappointment—expensive and dry.

YOUR WAY   You are trying to reduce the average cost of your meals. Turkey is cheaper per pound than other meats, so you buy some turkey parts (legs and breasts) as a substitute.

MY WAY   Turkey *is* cheaper per pound than other meats, but you can save even more money by buying a whole large frozen turkey instead of parts.

If you ask the butcher to cut the turkey into parts for you, chances are he'll say no because it is such a time-consuming job, and you must thaw the turkey first. So ask him first to cut the frozen turkey in half on his electric saw, then cut the halves into quarters, and finally into smaller pieces. If you approach him this way, he'll usually oblige.

You can then use the turkey parts for several meals. The breasts can be roasted whole or cut into steaks to make scallopini; the thighs can be cut into chunks for kabobs or creamed to go over noodles; and the legs and wings can be barbecued. Or you can roast half of the turkey and use the other half for other recipes or keep it frozen 'til you need it. And you still have plenty of scraps and bones left for soup.

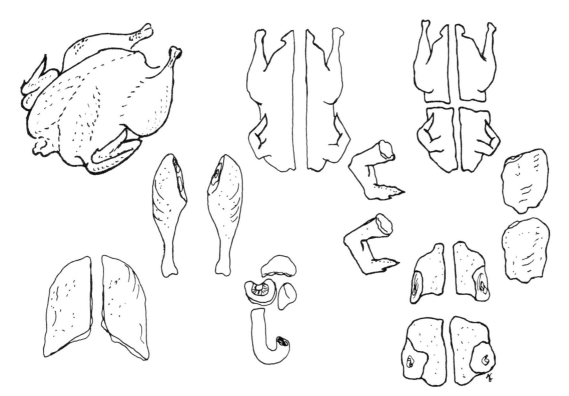

How to ask your butcher
to cut up a frozen turkey
on the electric saw:

Halves
Quarters
Then into pieces:
   drumsticks
   wings
   thighs
   breast pieces
   back pieces
   neck and innards

"Stretch your meat budget with turkey parts."

Use turkey breast steaks as a substitute for expensive veal:

To make turkey breast steaks, thoroughly chill the breast. Then cut across the grain.

TURKEY SCALLOPINI

1 lb.	turkey breast steaks	½ cup	butter
4 Tbsp.	grated Parmesan cheese	¼ lb.	fresh mushrooms, sliced
2 Tbsp.	flour	3 Tbsp.	chopped onion
1 tsp.	salt	¾ cup	dry white wine
¼ tsp.	pepper	1 cube	chicken bouillon (optional)
¼ tsp.	garlic salt		

(Pound turkey steak between pieces of waxed paper until thin.) Press into both sides of steaks a mixture of Parmesan cheese, flour and seasonings. Melt ¼ cup butter in skillet over medium heat. Saute steaks until golden brown, about 3 minutes on each side. Remove from skillet and keep warm. Saute mushrooms and onions in remaining butter; add wine and bouillon cube. Add browned turkey. Cover. Simmer 10 minutes or until tender. *4 servings.*

TURKEY PARMESAN

4	turkey breast steaks	1	egg, slightly beaten
½ cup	dry bread crumbs	¼ cup	salad oil
¼ cup	grated Parmesan cheese	1 can	(8 oz.) tomato sauce
salt and pepper		3 slices	Mozarella cheese, cut in strips
¼ tsp.	paprika		

In shallow pan, mix bread crumbs, cheese and spices. Dip turkey steaks in egg, then in crumb mixture. Heat oil in large skillet. Brown meat on both sides over medium heat until golden. Place steaks in baking dish. Pour on tomato sauce and arrange cheese on top. Bake until cheese is melted. Serve immediately. *4 servings.*

TERIYAKI TURKEY

2	turkey thighs

bottled teriyaki sauce

1	green pepper, cut in chunks
1	onion, cut in chunks

Bone thighs and remove skin. Cut meat into chunks. Marinate in teriyaki sauce for one hour at room temperature. Remove from sauce and place on skewers, alternating with pepper and onions. Barbecue or broil for ½ hour or until done. Turn while cooking and brush with remaining sauce. *4 servings.*

OVEN-BARBECUED TURKEY WINGS AND LEGS

2	each: turkey wings and thighs	1 tsp.	chili powder
1 tsp.	salt	½ tsp.	smoke salt or liquid smoke
2 Tbsp.	oil	¼ tsp.	pepper
1 can	(15 oz.) tomato sauce	1/8 tsp.	garlic powder
¼ cup	vinegar	1 can	(8 oz.) pineapple slices

Sprinkle turkey with salt. Brown slowly in heated oil. Pour off any fat in pan. Combine next 6 ingredients and ¼ cup syrup drained from pineapple slices. Pour over wings and heat to boiling. Cover. Bake in 350 degree oven for 1¼ hours, basting once or twice. Uncover, skim off any fat. Top each turkey piece with a pineapple slice. Bake, uncovered, 15 minutes longer. *4 servings.*

"Your best buy is a frozen, Grade A tom turkey."

Compare the cost of turkey parts and a whole turkey, using a 22-pound turkey as an example, to see how much you can save. Turkey parts are sold both fresh and frozen—again, your best buy is the frozen.

Turkey Part	Weight	Fresh Cost/lb.	Frozen Cost/lb.
Breast	7 lbs.	$1.99	$1.79
2 legs	4½ lbs.	$1.35	$0.59
2 thighs	4½ lbs.	$1.35	$1.15
2 wings	3 lbs.	$0.79	$0.59
1 neck & back	2½ lbs.	$0.79	$0.59
Gizzard, liver, heart	½ lb.	$0.99	$0.79

Total weight = 22 lbs.
Total cost/frozen = $24.00
Total cost/fresh = $30.93

But if you buy the whole turkey:

22 lbs. at $0.75 per lb. = $16.50

SAVINGS $14.43 (whole turkey instead of fresh parts) and
$ 7.50 (whole turkey instead of frozen parts)

YOUR WAY You've discovered many good recipes that use ground turkey, so you buy a pound.

1 lb. ground turkey at $1.09 per lb. = $1.09

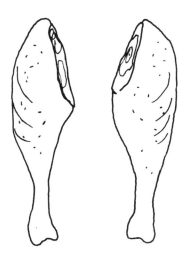

MY WAY I buy about 1¼ pounds of frozen turkey legs (the frozen legs are cheaper than fresh). I thaw them and bone them myself (very easy), then grind the meat at home. I save the bones, about ¼ pound, for soup stock, and I have 1 pound of ground turkey.

1¼ lb. turkey legs at $0.59 per lb. = $0.74

SAVINGS $0.35

TIP Ground turkey can be used in *any* recipe that calls for ground beef—and it's half the price! Try using ground turkey in meatloaf, burgers, hash, taco filling, skillet dinners, and sloppy joes. Here's a suggestion from one of my radio listeners: instead of ground beef, use a mixture of 3 parts ground turkey and 1 part pork sausage. The sausage adds a little flavor to the turkey—and they are both *much* cheaper than beef.

TURKEY LOAF

2 lbs.   fresh ground turkey
3 slices day-old bread, pulled
         into crumbs
2   eggs, slightly beaten
1   medium onion, minced
¼ cup minced green pepper
         (optional)

2 tbsp. prepared horseradish
2 tsp. salt
1 tsp. dry mustard
¼ cup evaporated milk
¾ cup catsup

Lightly mix all ingredients except ½ cup of the catsup. Mold in a 9x5x3-inch loaf pan. Spread top with remaining ½ cup catsup. Bake in a 375° oven for 1¼ hours. Pour juices from pan. Unmold loaf onto heated platter. If desired, use juices to make gravy. *8 servings*

TIP If you can't afford a whole turkey, consider buying a frozen turkey quarter roast. The forequarter roast consists of a half breast, a wing, and a portion of the giblets. It weighs 3 to 5 pounds and costs about $0.89 per pound.

The turkey hindquarter roast costs less, about $0.59 per pound, and includes the leg and thigh, as well as a portion of the giblets; weight is also 3 to 5 pounds.

TIP Frozen legs and wings are often very cheap. Watch for them. Ask the butcher to cut them into stew-size pieces (he can do this quickly on the electric saw). And you can sometimes buy turkey tails for as little as $0.39 per pound. You can make a delicious soup with them for pennies, or try baking them in the oven.

TURKEY STOCK

Delicious base for soups.

turkey carcass		1 tsp.	salt
½	medium carrot, sliced	2-3	celery leaves
½	medium onion, sliced	2-3	sprigs parsley
½ clove garlic, peeled		½	bay leaf

Place carcass in large kettle; cover with cold water. Add remaining ingredients. Cover; bring to a boil. Reduce heat and simmer 2 hours. Strain broth. Use at once or store in a closed jar in refrigerator 1 to 2 days. Or freeze for future use.

HEARTY TURKEY-VEGETABLE SOUP

4 cups	turkey stock	1 cup	chopped celery
½ cup	regular pearled barley	1 cup	sliced carrots
salt and pepper to taste		1 cup	canned whole kernel
2	small onions, chopped		corn, drained
½ cup	chopped parsley	2 cups	cooked, cubed turkey

Combine stock, barley, salt, pepper, onion and parsley in 3-quart saucepan. Bring to a boil; lower heat, cover and simmer 40 minutes, stirring occasionally. Add more stock if necessary. Add celery and carrots, cooking an additional 20 minutes, stirring frequently. Add corn and turkey; bring to a boil. Boil 2 minutes to heat through. *Serves 4.*

Cornish Hens

Cornish hens, sometimes called "game hens," are a good buy, especially when they're on sale. When you see a sale, stock up your freezer. Sometimes you'll see Cornish hens without a Grade A label; this is because they are missing a part—in some cases, the heart. The small print on the label tells you what's missing. These hens are just as good in quality, and you'll save some money.

TIP If you want to broil or barbecue Cornish hens, it's a good idea to have the butcher split the frozen hens in half, which he can easily do with his electric saw. Thaw them and they're ready for the grill. Or you can turn them skin-side down, stuff the cavity, wrap in tin foil, and bake. Remove foil for the last 20 minutes so they'll brown nicely.

Duck

Duck is not a popular item in this country. They are difficult to cook unless you are an expert. Watch for sales or for a Grade B duck, which will be cheaper because it's missing a part—leg or wing or giblets, or perhaps has a torn breast.

To save the most money when you buy poultry, remember these suggestions:

- Choose a large bird for the best yield,
- Never buy parts—buy a whole chicken or turkey and cut it up yourself,
- Watch for special buys on necks and backs—you can make a delicious soup for pennies,
- Don't pay more for a self-basting or stuffed turkey,
- Make you own ground turkey.

And be sure to stock up your freezer when prices are low; poultry freezes very well.

FISH

PEOPLE are eating more fish today as they become more diet and health conscious. Fish is good for you: It has as much protein as red meat, yet less fat and fewer calories. However, it is not the budget meal that it used to be. Prices are as high or higher than meat. To beat these high prices, there are things you should know: How to choose the best quality and the most economical form, and what kinds of fish are the best buys.

How to get the best quality for your dollar

Fish is not graded by the USDA but by the NOAA (National Oceanic and Atmospheric Administration), which is part of the U.S. Department of Commerce. However, only 15 percent of fishery products are inspected. Most fresh fish is not inspected because the consumer can see, touch, and smell the fish to determine its freshness, grading by eye. So you have to know what to look for.

The best way to make sure that a fish is fresh is to catch your own, but when the big ones get away and you head for the market, this is how to choose a fish that's fresh: Look for firm flesh (press it with your thumb); fresh and mild odor; bright, transparent eyes (protruding—not sunken in); reddish gills; and shiny skin. In frozen fish, beware of discoloration and strong odor. Know whether you're buying fresh or frozen, and if the fish is unsatisfactory, take it back!

TIP When you buy frozen fish, watch out for the label "breaded." This is not a good buy because you're paying 35 to 50 percent for the breading. Purchase the fish and bread it yourself by dipping it into beaten egg and then into a mixture of flour and bread crumbs with your favorite spices added.

The kinds of fish in the market

You'll see fish—fresh and frozen—sold in many different forms:

WHOLE As they come from the water. You can use about 60 percent of a fish once it is cleaned.

DRESSED Scales and entrails removed, and usually with the head, tail, and fins removed as well. It still has the bones and skin, but you can eat 80 percent of the fish. A small fish can be cooked this way, *pan dressed*.

STEAKS Cross-section slices. Once you remove the bones, you can use about 90 percent of the fish when it's cut in this form.

FILLETS Sides of the fish cut lengthwise away from the backbone.

A *butterfly fillet* is the two sides of the fish cut away from the backbone and held together by the uncut meat and skin of the belly. In this form you use 100 percent of the fish.

Chunks and portions are also cut from fresh fish or from frozen blocks of fish.

How much fish to buy for a meal

Remember that you don't have to buy as much fish as you do meat or poultry. It's a good value for your dollar because there is actually more edible meat per pound—no large chunks of fat, no big and heavy bones, and less fat to cook out. For example, to feed six people, most chefs would estimate 4 pounds of steak, 4½ pounds of pork, or 6 pounds of chicken, but just *three* pounds of fish fillets!

When you buy fish, don't forget *yield*, the ratio between meat and bone. A big fish will have better yield than a small one, so half a big fish is a better buy than a whole smaller fish. And, of course, some varieties of fish contain much more bone than others: mackerel and trout are examples of fish with many bones; swordfish and shark have few.

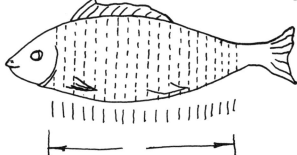 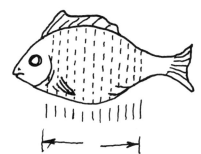

"A whole or half fish is cheaper than a fillet."

YOUR WAY You buy a fillet of salmon. It is in season, and although it's not cheap, you know it will be fresh and good.

> 1 lb. salmon fillet at $6.59 per lb. = $6.59

MY WAY I buy a whole or half fish and ask the butcher to remove the bone. If the whole or even half fish is too much, I buy the tail piece. I then ask the butcher to fillet it or cut it into steaks, or I do it myself. Even with the 40 percent waste in a whole fish, I come out ahead. I save the head, tail, and frame for soup stock. And my salmon fillet will cook out moister than yours because the juices won't run out.

> 1½ lbs. whole or half salmon at $3.59 per lb. = $5.38
> **SAVINGS** $1.21

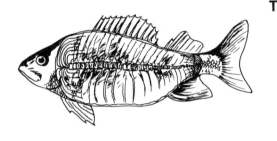

TIP Never throw away fish *frames* (the head, tail, and carcass); they make a delicious soup stock. You can buy these frames for a very low price ($0.59 per lb.). Sometimes you can get them free by going to the docks (like Fisherman's Wharf in San Francisco) or your local fishermen's wholesale market. As the fishermen clean their fish, they'll often give you the frames if you ask. You might even get a pretty good recipe out of them, too!

That's where I got this one:

FISH CHOWDER

Stock:

Put 2 fish frames in some cheesecloth; tie in a knot. Place in a large kettle of water and cook with some vegetables (carrots, onions) for several hours. Squeeze out the cheesecloth and discard the whole thing. You'll end up with the best-flavored fish stock you've ever tasted.

To the stock, add some chopped onions, garlic, and parsley; diced carrots, potatoes, and celery; fresh tomatoes; and some meaty pieces of fish. Season with salt and pepper and a bay leaf or two. Cook until the vegetables are tender. Serve with French bread. A fantastic meal for very little money!

TIP   Another bargain is fish *collars.* This piece, from behind the head around the gills, has a lot of meat and sells for a reasonable price.

The most important rule in saving money when you buy fish is to watch for sales and know what's in season. There is a great variety of fish available: 240 commercial species of fish and shellfish are marketed in the United States today. Most varieties of fresh fish have a certain season, and during this time they are cheaper and more abundant. Ask your dealer about the species available and the ones most plentiful where you live. Your best buy will usually be local fish in season.

You will sometimes see good buys on fish that has been farmed rather than caught. Catfish is raised on farms in the Midwest, and in the Northwest there are trout farms. The fish is flown in fresh and sold at good prices. Watch for the metal tag on trout that tells you where it was raised.

Try this simple recipe for trout:

BAKED TROUT

Butter the trout; sprinkle on some sherry, dill, salt and pepper. Wrap in aluminum foil and bake at 350 degrees for 25 to 30 minutes. Open foil for the last ten minutes so the fish can brown. This makes a wonderful brunch!

TIP Don't forget canned fish. Tuna, salmon, and sardines are often a good buy per pound and have the advantage of never spoiling.

Be adventurous and try different kinds of fish! Lesser-known species are often as tasty as the popular species and are usually cheaper. I have several varieties to suggest in the following pages.

YOUR WAY You buy fresh swordfish steaks—an excellent fish, but very expensive.

1 lb. at $6.99 per lb. = $6.99

MY WAY I buy some shark steaks for less than a third the price of swordfish. I cook them the same way you'd cook your swordfish and the taste is so similar, I bet I could fool you.

1 lb. shark at $2.09 per lb. = $2.09
SAVINGS $4.90

TIP Cut shark meat with a round cookie cutter or center section from a doughnut cutter and serve as scallops. Some restaurants do this and you probably never know it! I'd suggest using soupfin shark, and for added flavor, marinate the "scallops" in clam juice for about six hours.

More and more people are discovering shark, so don't be afraid to try it. It has no bones (other than a spine), a firm texture, and a mild taste. And it's so inexpensive! It can be used in almost any recipe that calls for lean fish and is especially good to barbecue on skewers because it is firm and will not fall apart. You can even marinate shark—try it in teriyaki sauce.

Shark is available fresh or frozen throughout the year and is usually sold as steaks and fillets. Commonly marketed species are leopard, soupfin, and thresher. (The fins of soupfin shark are used for shark-fin soup, a Chinese delicacy.)

SHARK TERIYAKI

2 lbs.	fresh shark fillets, cut in 1 inch chunks
1 can	(16 oz.) pineapple chunks
½ cup	soy sauce
¼ cup	sherry (optional)
2 Tbsp.	brown sugar
1 tsp.	ground ginger or fresh ginger grated
1 tsp.	dry mustard
1 clove	garlic, crushed
1	green pepper, cut in 1 inch squares
	Cherry tomatoes, mushrooms, onions (optional)
	Bamboo or metal skewers

Drain pineapple chunks reserving ¼ cup of juice. Make marinade by combining pineapple juice, soy sauce, sherry, brown sugar, ginger, mustard and garlic. Pour marinade over fish chunks. Cover and refrigerate fish for at least 1 hour. Drain fish and reserve marinade. Thread fish chunks, pineapple chunks and green pepper squares alternately on skewers. Include cherry tomatoes, fresh mushrooms and onion wedges if desired. Cook over hot coals or under broiler about 4 inches from source of heat for 5 minutes. Baste with marinade. Turn and cook for 5 minutes more or until fish flakes easily when tested with a fork. Serve as a main dish on a bed of rice or alone as an hors d'oeuvre. Makes 6 entree servings or 18 to 20 hors d'oeuvres.

Skate

Skate is another species of fish that is delicious and economical, but not well known. Usually only the wings and fins are marketed, with the skin removed. If you catch your own skate, cut the wings into chunks and blanch with boiling water so the skin can be peeled off easily. Skate has a delicate texture and flavor. Like shark, it can be used in any recipe that calls for lean fish. Try it broiled, baked, fried, poached, grilled, smoked, served with a sauce, or added to soups, chowders, and gumbos.

OVEN-FRIED SKATE

2 lbs. skate wings	1 cup fine bread crumbs
½ cup milk	⅓ cup cooking oil or melted fat
1½ Tbsp. salt	

Wipe chunks of skate wings with a damp cloth and dry thoroughly. Add salt to milk; stir until dissolved. Dip first in milk, then in bread crumbs, and place on a greased shallow baking pan. Top each piece of fish with oil or melted fat, and bake in a preheated oven at 375° for 25 minutes.

Catfish

In the Midwest, catfish used to be considered junk fish. Now it's
enjoying a great revival. Catfish farms are now a big industry,
primarily in the Mississippi delta area. The fish can be found
inexpensively at many stores. Pan dressed or in steaks, catfish is
traditionally served at fish fries, accompanied by coleslaw and
hush puppies (fried cornbread dumplings).

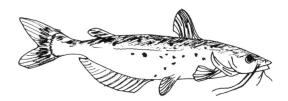

CATFISH GUMBO

1 lb.	skinned catfish fillets, fresh or frozen	1 can	(1 lb.) tomatoes
½ cup	chopped celery	1 pkg.	(10 oz.) frozen okra or fresh okra, sliced
½ cup	chopped green pepper	2 tsp.	salt
½ cup	chopped onion	¼ tsp.	pepper
1 clove	garlic, finely chopped	¼ tsp.	thyme
¼ cup	melted fat or oil	1	whole bay leaf
2 cubes	beef bouillon	Dash liquid hot pepper sauce	
2 cups	boiling water	1½ cups hot cooked rice	

Cut fillets into one-inch pieces. Cook celery, green pepper, onion, and garlic in fat until tender. Dissolve bouillon cubes in water. Add bouillon, tomatoes, okra, and seasonings. Cover and simmer for 30 minutes. Add fish. Cover and simmer for 15 minutes longer or until fish flakes easily when tested with a fork. Remove bay leaf. Place ¼ cup rice in each of 6 soup bowls. Fill with gumbo. *Serves 6.*

Squid

Squid also is growing in popularity as consumers become aware of its economy and versatility as a food. Like clams and oysters, it is a mollusk and is found on both coasts. It is available either fresh or frozen for a very low price. You can save even more by buying a 5-pound frozen box of squid, from which you can break off a piece at a time without having to thaw the whole thing.

The only complicated part about squid is learning to clean it. But with these instructions, you can do it.

PREPARING SQUID

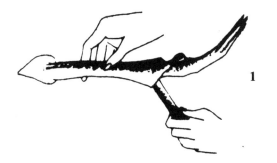

1   Cut the mantle of the squid lengthwise with a knife.

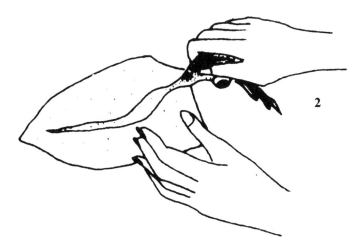

2   Spread open the inside of the mantle, press flat, and pull off the head and arms of the squid, removing the intestines at the same time.

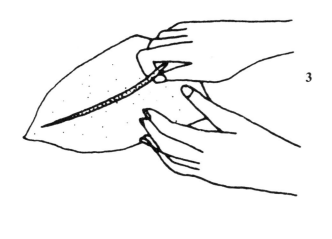

3   Pull out the transparent
     backbone and any remain-
     ing viscera.

4   Turn mantle to other side.
     Starting with the tail end,
     pinch the fins, pulling off
     the fins and speckled outer
     membrane. Wash the
     squid. Cut the mantle into
     strips or pieces.

5   A squid has two tentacles
     and eight arms. To prepare
     them for cooking, cut
     across the head in front of
     the eyes. Squeeze out the
     round sac containing the
     beak. The skin can be
     pulled off the arms after
     they have been placed in
     boiling water for 2 or 3
     minutes, or you can leave
     it on.

Squid can be marinated raw, cut into rings and fried, sauteed, boiled to be used in salads, baked, or used in stew. On the west coast, fish markets feature rounds of squid they call *abalonette.* These rounds sell for about $2.98 a pound. Buy whole squid at $0.95 a pound and make your own rounds!

When it is pounded and quickly fried, squid tastes very much like the expensive delicacy, abalone, which sells for over $25 a pound.

TIP Squid can be tenderized by pounding with a mallet, or by soaking in hot water for ten minutes.

FRIED SQUID

2 lbs.	squid, fresh or frozen	2 Tbsp.	milk
2 Tbsp.	lemon juice	½ cup	flour
salt and pepper		½ cup	bread crumbs
1	egg, beaten	oil for frying	

Clean squid, cut into pieces. Sprinkle with lemon juice and salt and pepper. Combine milk and egg in one bowl; flour and bread crumbs in another. Dip squid in milk and egg, then in flour mixture. Fry quickly in hot oil, turning once. (Overcooking makes squid tough; when it curls up on the ends, it's done.) Drain. Serve with lemon wedges and tartar sauce. *3-4 servings.*

SAUTEED SQUID

2 lbs.	squid, cleaned and cut into strips	2 Tbsp.	chopped parsley
3 Tbsp.	butter	1 Tbsp.	lemon juice
1 tsp.	minced garlic		dash of white wine
½ cup	mushrooms, sliced		dash salt and pepper

Melt butter in a 9-inch skillet. Saute garlic and mushrooms (optional) 1 minute. Add squid and remaining ingredients and saute 30 seconds to 1 minute over medium high heat until squid loses its transparent look and curls up. *4 servings.*

SQUID MARINARA

2 lbs.	squid, fresh or frozen	1 can	(1 lb. 12 oz.) tomatoes
1 clove	garlic, crushed	2 Tbsp.	chopped parsley
2 Tbsp.	cooking or olive oil	½ tsp.	oregano
½ tsp.	salt	1 pkg.	(8 oz.) spaghetti

Clean squid and cut mantle and tentacles into 1 inch pieces. Cook squid and garlic in hot oil for 5 minutes, stirring occasionally. Press tomatoes through a strainer. Add tomatoes, parsley, oregano and salt; stir. Cover and simmer for approximately 10 minutes longer. Cook spaghetti as directed on package. Serve over spaghetti. *4 to 6 servings.*

Abalone

If you're trying to save money, don't bother even looking at abalone. It's tasty, but who can afford it! Instead, try my recipe for "phony abalone." This recipe has even fooled patrons at a fine seafood restaurant. A San Francisco restaurant served this phony abalone for several years. Fearing discovery, they began using real abalone, but got so many customer complaints, they switched back!

PHONY ABALONE

2 boneless chicken breasts
1 bottle clam juice
fresh garlic

Take boneless chicken breasts (remember to buy the whole chicken, cut up and freeze the rest), remove the skin, and slice into steaks. Place steaks between waxed paper and pound thin. Pour clam juice over the chicken, add fresh garlic, to taste. Cover and refrigerate for 36 hours. Drain the chicken, dip in egg, then a flour/bread-crumb mixture and fry quickly. Serve with lemon wedges and tartar sauce. And don't tell your friends it's chicken!

DON'T THROW AWAY THE CLAM JUICE! Use it to make a delicious clam chowder to serve with dinner. Put the juice in a saucepan, add diced potato and celery, pepper and salt, 1 can baby clams. Add milk for white chowder; fresh tomatoes or tomato sauce for red chowder.

Shellfish

Shellfish is very expensive. The best way to save money is to buy when it is in season and is most plentiful. So always watch for sales. Also, check to see if frozen shrimp is available in 5-pound boxes at a lower price.

When you buy a whole crab, here's how to choose the best one. If two crabs are about the same size, always buy the heavier one. A crab grows until it fills its shell, then it pops out and grows a new shell. You pay for the same amount of shell anyway, so you get more meat in the heavier crab.

TIP To stretch a crab salad or casserole, take cooked halibut, chilled and shredded from the bones, and add it to the crab meat, then put it in the salad. You won't be able to tell which is which, and halibut is a lot less expensive than crab.

Fish *can* be a budget meal when you remember these tips:

- Buy less fish than you would meat or poultry—fish has more edible meat per pound.
- Know your best buys—the local fish in season.
- Get a whole or half fish instead of steaks or fillets.
- Buy fish frames or collars for an economical soup.
- Try different kinds of fish—shark, skate, squid.
- And try my "phony abalone."

SMOKED MEAT

SMOKED meat is delicious, but it is more expensive than fresh meat because you're paying for an additional process, the smoking. Still, I have a few tips for you that will help you save money when you buy smoked meats. If you really like meat prepared this way, you might consider smoking it yourself at home. You don't have to have an expensive smoker—you can use your oven or barbecue grill. There are also some short cuts by using liquid smoke—it can do wonders.

Ham, bacon, and Canadian bacon can be purchased in just about any supermarket, but other smoked meats—tongue, spareribs, turkey, fish—are harder to find. Gourmet shops often carry them, but at gourmet prices. If you can't find the smoked meat you want, ask your butcher and he can order it for you. But the best bargains are when you make it yourself.

Bacon

YOUR WAY You buy a package of sliced bacon, paying a medium price—neither the cheapest nor most expensive. You hope it's nice and lean but, with the slices overlapped, you can't really tell.

1 lb. sliced bacon at $1.29 per lb. = $1.29

MY WAY I buy a pound of slab bacon. It is easy to see how lean it is. And it is fresh—not sliced weeks ago.

I ask the butcher to slice it for me, leaving on the rind—which I happen to like. The rind is usually removed on packaged, sliced bacon. Or, even better, I slice it at home, either by hand or using my meat slicer. That way I slice only the amount I need and the rest will stay fresh and not dry out.

1 lb. slab bacon at $0.99 per lb. = $0.99
SAVINGS $0.30 per lb.

Not only do you save money, you get what you want when you want it, you don't waste anything, and you don't have a big, bulky package or plastic wrapping getting in the way of everything else in your refrigerator.

"Bacon—without salt, sugar, or preservatives."

TIP Here are some substitutes for expensive sliced bacon:

Bacon ends and pieces can often be bought far cheaper and are ideal for flavoring vegetables. The lean pieces can be put in omelettes.

Smoked jowl is much cheaper than sliced bacon but has that good bacon flavor. Your butcher can order it for you if he doesn't have it on hand.

TIP If you're worried about eating salt, sugar, and nitrites, you can make your own bacon—*without* salt, sugar, or any of the other preservatives! Here's what to do: Buy fresh pork belly—not always easy to find, but your butcher can always order it for you. You can also use salt pork if you wash out all the salt by running hot water over it for five minutes. Slice it thin and baste with a mixture of honey and liquid smoke, then cook as you would bacon. Delicious! Another way to cook it is to roll the slices in egg and cracker meal, then fry them. This is a real southern delicacy.

Canadian bacon

YOUR WAY You buy Canadian bacon, sliced and vacuum packed. (Canadian bacon is the boneless section of the pork loin, smoked.)

1 lb. sliced Canadian bacon at $6.08 per lb. = $6.08

MY WAY Canadian bacon is not cheap, but I can save by buying a chunk of it instead of slices. I cut off slices as I use them, and the rest stays fresh and doesn't dry out. A chunk of Canadian bacon is also good baked in the oven.

1 lb. chunk Canadian bacon at $3.39 per lb. = $3.39
SAVINGS $2.69

Ham

YOUR WAY You buy three center-cut ham slices, about a pound each.

3 lbs. at $2.99 per lb. = $8.97

MY WAY I buy a shank half of ham, which weighs about 9 pounds, and ask the butcher to cut off about three center slices. (I buy a *half,* not just a portion, because the center slices will have already been taken off the shank portion.) I get my three slices, plus a 6-pound ham to bake, not to mention bones for flavoring soup.

3 lbs. center cuts at $1.89 per lb. = $5.67

SAVINGS $1.10 per lb.
or $3.30 for 3 lbs.

If you can use it, a whole ham (about 13–16 lbs.) is also a good buy. However, remember that ham does not freeze well. Ask your butcher to cut 3 pounds of center slices, a 5-pound shank-end portion, a 4-pound butt-end portion, and 1 pound of ham hocks.

TIP The shank portion is a better buy than the butt portion because you can get more steaks from the shank. Remember, for the best yield (the most meat for your money), always choose the largest portion, or the half or whole ham.

1 Butt roast

2 Steaks

3 Shank-leg roast

4 Shank pieces (hock)

"A picnic ham is your best buy."

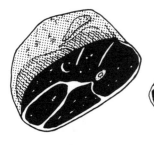

Butt portion   **Shank portion**

YOUR WAY   You buy a ham portion.

7 lbs. ham portion at $1.69 per lb. = $11.83

MY WAY   I buy a picnic shoulder. The difference is this: the ham is the rear leg; the picnic is the shoulder. The picnic is much less expensive, and the meat is sweeter than that of the leg. I choose the largest picnic available because the yield is better.

7 lbs. picnic at $1.29 per lb. = $9.03
SAVINGS $2.80

TIP   Pour a can of 7-Up over the ham, place in the oven, and baste frequently. Delicious!

TIP Also try a smoked pork butt. It is a tasty, delicious boneless piece of meat, with very little waste. It's not as cheap as a picnic shoulder, but it's quite reasonable.

YOUR WAY You buy some diced ham. What you don't know is that the reason it is being sold diced is because it didn't sell as a slice. It is discolored on one side, and a bit dried out. Both these effects come from being exposed too long to the air.

1 lb. diced ham at $2.79 per lb. = $2.79

MY WAY I buy ham hocks, cut the meat off the bone, dice it, and it's ready to use in a casserole or salad. I save the bones for soup, or to flavor string beans. My diced ham is pink and juicy, and costs less than half what you pay.

1 lb. ham hocks at $1.29 per lb. = $1.29
SAVINGS $1.50

Ham / 181

YOUR WAY   You buy a package of sliced ham for sandwiches.

4 oz. ham slices at $1.39 (You're paying $5.56 per pound!)

MY WAY   I buy a canned ham. There are several brands and sizes to choose from; so before I make my decision, I check the unit prices to see how much I pay per pound. If the store does not mark the unit prices, I divide the number of pounds into the selling prices to find out the price per pound. A pocket calculator does this in seconds. Then I can choose the best buy.

A butcher will usually slice a ham as a free service. If not, you can do it yourself at home.

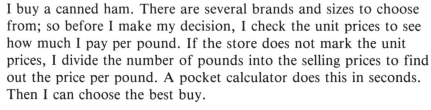

Canned ham at $3.29 per pound
SAVINGS $2.27 per pound

TIP   Buying a canned ham is like buying a pig in a poke. Save your receipt. If you are not satisfied, take it back and get your money back.

TIP   Watch out for coupons that say "$2.00 off the price of any size canned ham." Sometimes the ham is priced so high that even after you take off the $2.00, it's still no bargain. Compare prices so you won't be fooled.

Luncheon meats

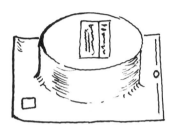

YOUR WAY You buy some packaged sliced salami for sandwiches and snacks.

3 oz. = $1.09 or $5.76 per lb.

MY WAY I buy a chub salami. They usually come in half-pound and pound sizes. If I'm going to use it all at once, I ask the butcher to slice it for me. In most stores they do this for no additional charge. If I'm not going to use it all right away, I slice it myself as I need. That way it stays fresh and doesn't dry out.

1 lb. chub salami = $4.70
SAVINGS $1.06

TIP On any lunch meat, it's cheaper to buy a chub or chunk and slice it yourself. But remember that luncheon meats should not be frozen. Buy only as much as you can use quickly.

"Smoking that's good for your health."

Smoking meat at home

There's more to smoked meat than ham, bacon, and luncheon meat. Smoked chicken, turkey, pork chops, spareribs, tongue, and fish are different and delicious—but they can be very expensive, and you may have to go to a gourmet shop to get them.

You can smoke your own meat at home, and you don't need an expensive smoker to do it. All you need is a hooded barbecue, or if you don't have one of these, you can smoke meat in your oven.

Using your hooded barbecue: Soak hickory chips in water, then spread a thin layer over hot coals; add more chips as needed. Or you can place a hot plate instead of coals in the bottom of the barbecue, and put the hickory chips in an iron skillet on top of the hot plate. This way it is easier to keep the heat low and constant. Put the hood on the barbecue and cook the meat slowly, for about two hours. (Before smoking fish, marinate it in brine for about an hour.)

You can also get a wonderful smoked flavor by using bottled liquid smoke, which is available in any supermarket. There are no chemicals in it—it's pure natural smoke from hickory wood, trapped as it is formed, condensed, and then bottled. Sprinkle this liquid smoke on your charcoal coals when they are hot. Cover the barbecue and cook the meat slowly. Or you can rub the meat with liquid smoke and place in a plastic bag in the refrigerator over-night. Cook the meat in your oven, or any way you like—it will have a lovely, smoky flavor.

Try also using liquid smoke to flavor ground meat. Use no more than one teaspoonful to 5 pounds of meat—too much will give the meat a bad taste.

SMOKED SPARERIBS

Brush liquid smoke on both sides of the spareribs (small spareribs are the best). Place in plastic bag and refrigerate overnight. Remove from bag, brush on more liquid smoke, and bake in the oven at 325° for the required length of time. Place on cutting board and cut between the ribs. Serve with chilled applesauce.

When buying smoked meat:

- Don't buy pre-sliced bacon, Canadian bacon, ham, or lunch meat;
- Watch for bargains, such as bacon ends and pieces, and smoked jowl;
- Buy a half or whole ham, not center slices or portions;
- Know your best buy in ham—the picnic shoulder;
- Do your own smoking at home;
- Try flavoring fresh meat with liquid smoke.

This way you'll have delicious smoked meat on your menu, and some money left in your pocket.

VARIETY MEATS

VARIETY MEATS—brains, hearts, kidneys, liver, sweetbreads, tripe, tongue—are protein bargains. There is no bone, little waste, little or no fat, and the price is reasonable. There is not a large supply of these meats, but the price is still reasonable because they are less in demand. Many consumers are not familiar with them and don't know how to prepare them.

BRAINS Calf brains are the best, and the most expensive. Beef brains are very similar and are about 20 cents less per pound. Lamb brains are 20 cents less than beef. Soak brains in vinegar water, then blanch them before cooking and pull off the outer membrane. Brains are one of the most perishable organ meats, so use them immediately after you buy them. Try brains scrambled with eggs, or saute or bake them.

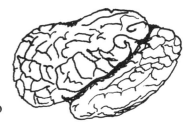

SWEETBREADS are considered a delicacy, and higher demand means higher price. These glands (from the throat) are a lot like brains in taste and texture. Veal sweetbreads are the most popular (and of course, most expensive). Soak, blanch, and peel sweetbreads as you would brains.

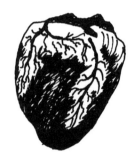

HEART is plentiful and reasonably priced. Beef and calf hearts cost more than lamb or beef. Don't pay more for sliced heart—buy it whole and slice it yourself. Heart can be baked or fried; it can also be stuffed or added to a stew. Try adding it to ground meat—an inexpensive way to stretch ground beef or lamb.

KIDNEYS are inexpensive and can be cooked a variety of ways. Beef and veal kidneys are the best buy; lamb kidneys are more expensive. Try making a kidney pie, or broil veal kidneys alongside small veal loin chops.

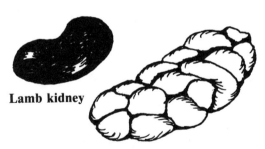

Lamb kidney

Beef kidney

LIVER is always available. Try lamb and pork liver. They are not as popular as beef or calf, but are quite similar in taste—and much cheaper. Pork liver is the most nutritious. Ask the butcher to skin the liver; it will be a lot less chewy. Chicken livers are also a good buy.

POLYNESIAN PORK LIVER

1 lb.	pork liver, cut ½-inch thick	3 Tbsp.	pineapple juice
4 slices	bacon	2 Tbsp.	cider vinegar
⅓ cup	chopped onion	½ tsp.	dried basil
⅓ cup	pineapple chunks	½ tsp.	dried thyme
¼ cup	chopped green pepper	salt	
½ cup	packed brown sugar	pepper	

In medium skillet, cook bacon over moderate heat until crisp. Remove bacon; reserve drippings in skillet. Crumble bacon and reserve. Add onion, pineapple, and green pepper to reserved drippings. Cook, stirring occasionally, over moderate heat until onion and green pepper are tender. Stir in brown sugar, pineapple juice, vinegar, basil, thyme, and reserved bacon. Season to taste with salt and pepper. Place liver in 12 x 7½ x 2-inch baking dish. Pour sauce over liver. Bake in 350 degree oven until liver is done, about 25 minutes. *4 servings*.

Honeycomb tripe

TRIPE is the wall of stomach in beef. Honeycomb tripe is best (most tender), but you pay more for it. You may have to order it in advance. Tripe is the main ingredient in Philadelphia pepper pot soup. Try tripe with pigs feet—a delicious meal.

PIGS FEET AND TRIPE

(Theresa Pieretti, Sonoma, California)

5 lbs.	tripe	½ tsp.	thyme
2	pigs feet, each cut into three pieces	½ tsp.	oregano
		3 cans	tomato sauce
1	large onion	1 cup	sauterne
parsley		1 cup	chicken broth
3 cloves	garlic	2	bay leaves
1	small chili pepper		parmesan cheese
8	peppercorns		oil

Cut tripe into thin strips. Parboil tripe and pigs feet 20 to 25 minutes. Rinse with warm water and set aside. Heat oil in a saucepan, add chopped onion, garlic and parsley. Saute for 15 minutes. Add thyme, oregano, tomato sauce, wine, broth and bay leaves; then add meat, peppercorns, and chili pepper. Cover and cook for an hour and a half. Sprinkle Parmesan cheese on each serving. *Serves 6.*

TONGUE Beef and calf tongue are the most popular and are usually available; lamb tongue may have to be ordered in advance. After cooking tongue, peel off the skin before serving. Make a tongue pot roast and use the leftovers for sandwiches. Tasty!

BEEF TONGUE, SPANISH STYLE OR "BEEF BONANZA"

(This is my wife Dee's recipe, and it's so delicious you can't eat just one helping. Some people don't like tongue, so I call it "Beef Bonanza" and they love it!)

1	8 oz. can tomato sauce	1	fresh beef tongue
2	pinches oregano	1	large onion, chopped
1 tsp.	chili powder	3 cloves garlic, minced	
salt and pepper to taste		3 tbsp. parsley, chopped	

Rinse tongue in cold water. Place in large pot and cover with water. Bring to a boil, then turn down heat and simmer 1½ to 2 hours.

While tongue is cooking, make the sauce. Saute onion in skillet in small amount of oil. Add garlic and parsley and saute a few more minutes. Stir in tomato sauce and one can of water. Add spices, cover and cook on low heat for 45 minutes.

Remove tongue from pot, place on cutting board and peel off the skin. Cut away the tiny bones and excess fat at the large end, and slice the tongue ¼-inch thick. Place slices in the sauce and simmer for 20 minutes with cover on; then remove cover and cook another 15 minutes to thicken the sauce. Add salt and pepper to taste.

Pet Food

When you buy canned or packaged pet food, you can pay as much as $1.00 per pound. It's a lot cheaper to make your own, and these savings will add up!

Buy fresh beef kidneys for about 79 cents per lb. or beef melts (spleens) at only 49 cents per lb. You can save even more by ordering a case of melts (about 30 pounds). Divide into smaller packages and put in your freezer. To insure getting beef melts, order them at least 3 days in advance.

Grind or chop the kidneys or melts and mix with leftover vegetables and/or cereal for a superior pet food.

Ask your butcher if he'll save liver trimmings for you; also fish trimmings for your cat.

You can also cook chicken innards and scraps for your animals, but be sure not to give them the bones, which can damage your pet's intestines and stomach lining.

"Smile when you put meat in the freezer and laugh all the way to the bank."

Conclusion—Start Saving!

Now that you have read the book, take a little inventory of your shopping habits. Have you changed? Are you saving money now, when you missed the boat before?

I hope this book helps you, the consumer. You are paying the bills, and I think you have the right to know how to get the most for your money. I hope that now you have a better knowledge of how to shop and save:

- by recognizing the good buys,
- by choosing the best quality meat,
- by knowing how to ask the butcher to cut and bone the meat you buy,
- by cutting and grinding meat at home,
- by stocking your freezer, and
- by trying money-saving recipes.

Let me know how "My Way" works for you. Write to Reggie the Butcher, Petaluma, California 94952 (that's all you need—the letter will get to me).

Good luck and good savings.

INDEX